Making Gourd Headpieces

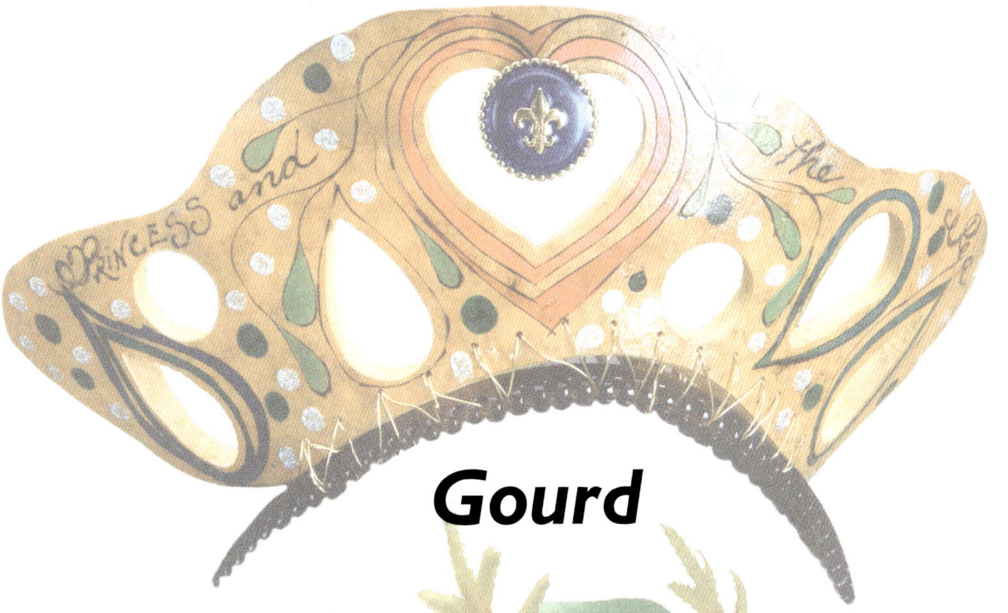

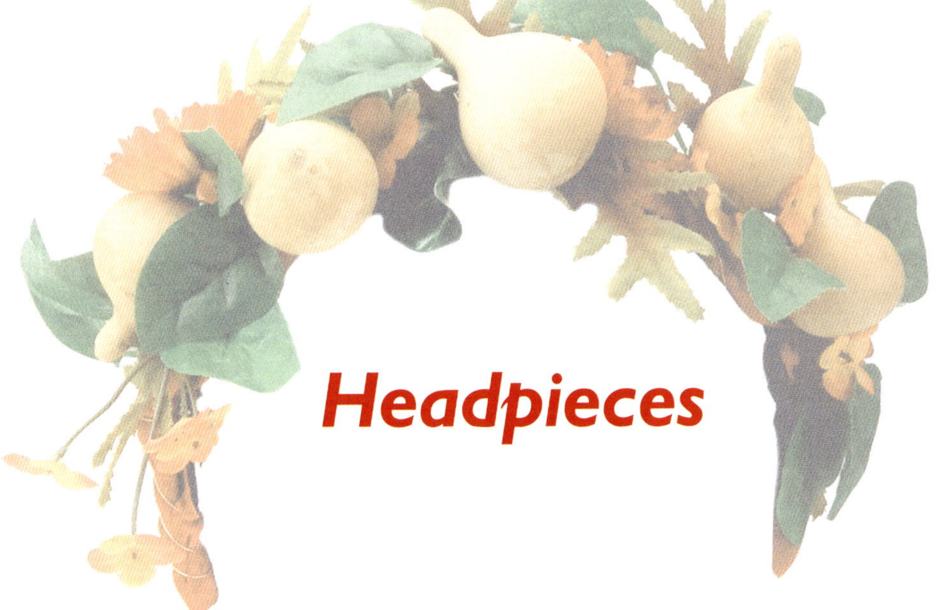

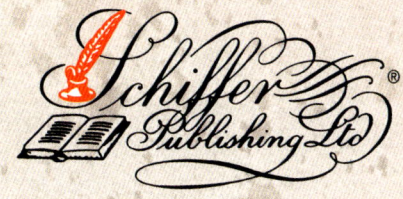

C. Angela Mohr

4880 Lower Valley Road, Atglen, PA 19310

Other Schiffer Books by C. Angela Mohr
Gourd Puppets and Dolls, 978-0-7643-2868-8, $14.95
Gourd Ornaments for Holiday Decorating, 978-0-7643-2716-2, $12.95
Gourd Art Basics, 978-0-7643-2829-9, $14.95
Historic Gourd Crafts, 978-0-7643-2830-5, $14.95

Other Schiffer Books on Related Subjects
Gourd Crafts, 978-0-7643-2825-1, $14.95

Schiffer Books are available at special discounts for bulk purchases for sales promotions or premiums. Special editions, including personalized covers, corporate imprints, and excerpts can be created in large quantities for special needs. For more information contact the publisher:

Published by Schiffer Publishing Ltd.
4880 Lower Valley Road
Atglen, PA 19310
Phone: (610) 593-1777; Fax: (610) 593-2002
E-mail: Info@schifferbooks.com

For the largest selection of fine reference books on this and related subjects, please visit our web site at **www.schifferbooks.com**
We are always looking for people to write books on new and related subjects. If you have an idea for a book please contact us at the above address.

This book may be purchased from the publisher.
Include $3.95 for shipping.
Please try your bookstore first.
You may write for a free catalog.

In Europe, Schiffer books are distributed by
Bushwood Books
6 Marksbury Ave.
Kew Gardens
Surrey TW9 4JF England
Phone: 44 (0) 20 8392-8585; Fax: 44 (0) 20 8392-9876
E-mail: info@bushwoodbooks.co.uk
Website: www.bushwoodbooks.co.uk
Free postage in the U.K., Europe; air mail at cost.

Copyright © 2008 by C. Angela Mohr
Library of Congress Control Number: 2007941799

All rights reserved. No part of this work may be reproduced or used in any form or by any means—graphic, electronic, or mechanical, including photocopying or information storage and retrieval systems—without written permission from the publisher.
The scanning, uploading and distribution of this book or any part thereof via the Internet or via any other means without the permission of the publisher is illegal and punishable by law. Please purchase only authorized editions and do not participate in or encourage the electronic piracy of copyrighted materials.
"Schiffer," "Schiffer Publishing Ltd. & Design," and the "Design of pen and ink well" are registered trademarks of Schiffer Publishing Ltd.

Designed by RoS
Type set in Humanst521 BT

ISBN: 978-0-7643-2869-5
Printed in China

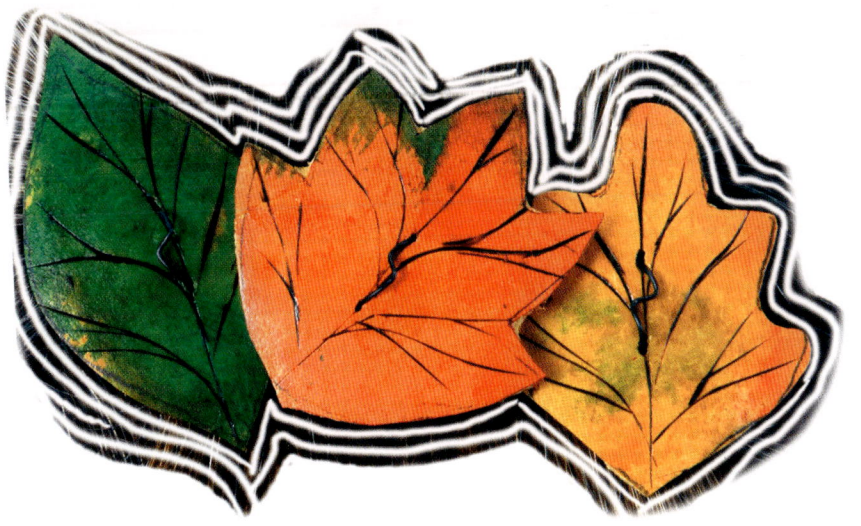

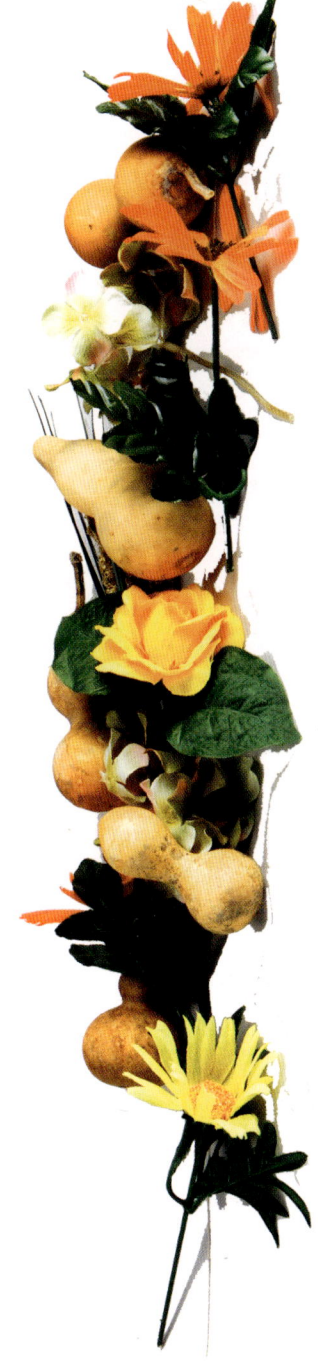

What's Inside

Dedication..4

Introduction:...5
    Calling all Gourd Heads! 5

Chapter One: Preparation.......................6
    Gourds to Use 6
    Equipment 7

Chapter Two: Tiara..................................8
    Full Wrap 17
    Comb 19

Chapter Three: Harvest Head................21
    Headband 21
    Hatband 29
    Caplet 33
    Hatpin 36

Chapter Four: Barrettes.........................39
    A Gourd Barrette 39
    A Gourd-decorated Barrette 42
    A Leafy Idea 46

Chapter Five: Thinking Cap....................50
    Full Cap 50
    Light Bulb 56

Concluding Words..................................59

Gallery..60

Dedication

Dedicated to my sister Kimberly, this book is about Princesses who grew up to become the Queens and Heroes of the people in their lives. All around us are special folks who make a difference in the world with their day-to-day words and actions and points of view. These are the Queens of action, these are the Heroes of positive change, these are the people who make the world a better place by sowing the seeds of betterment one thought, one action, one attitude at a time. Kimberly is my hero.

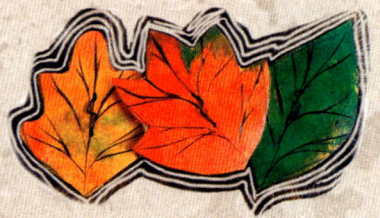

Introduction:

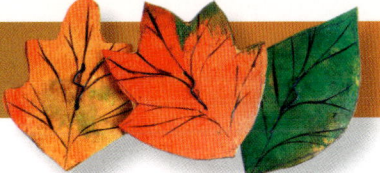

Calling all Gourd Heads!

Too often a gourd enthusiast accumulates pieces of gourds left over from other projects. What to do, what to do? These pieces are exciting because with just a little imagination, they can become big ideas for small projects. This book is a springboard of small projects you can do to make use of leftover pieces or, if you get inspired, to plan for a whole gourd.

You will need cleaned pieces of gourd. If you have pieces of past projects, they are probably already cleaned and ready to go. If not, you need a quick primer to get ready.

First, a gourd for craft or art purposes needs to be dehydrated. A fresh gourd off the vine in autumn will be eighty percent, or more, moisture, and all that moisture needs to be dehydrated. That process can take two or more seasons in a well-ventilated area. In fact, I leave mine on the vine all winter and early spring so the passing winds can whisk away the moisture. When the gourd is ready, it will look cruddy: peeling, molded, gross. But, as long as it held its shape, sounds hollow when tapped, and is lightweight for its size, the gourd should be good to use! Dampen the surface with water and scrub the surface crud with a metal pot scrubbie. If you make a tiara or barrette, you will want to open the gourd with a carpet knife or jigsaw to scrape away the interior debris and sand the interior to a smooth finish. Remember to wear a mask or, better, a respirator because gourd dust is toxic!

Once the gourds, or pieces of gourd, are ready to use, any art media can be utilized to decorate them to your liking. I like to use a woodburner, permanent markers, nail polish, and papercuttings to make my designs because those are the things I have in the house and garage. However, you may have other stuff around that you like to use: crayons, color pencils, press-on decals, etc. A spray-on laquer will seal almost anything, but other sealants also work well, so be open to different ideas. Headpieces are supposed to be fun — and having fun making them just enhances the wonderful gourdiness all around!

Chapter One:

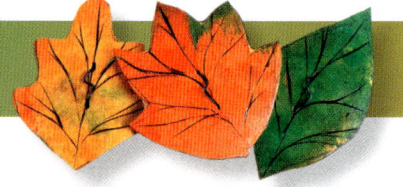

Preparation

Gourds to Use

All the gourds for this book have already been washed. I am using pieces of kettle gourds, dipper gourds, and mini-bottleneck gourds. Depending on the size of the gourd, the leftover pieces will have different curves. The amount of curve to the piece will determine what can be made in some cases. For example, a large gourd (10" diameter belly) will produce a piece with a big enough curve that a full tiara can be made because it will fit the curve of a head. A piece of a small gourd will have a smaller, tighter curve, making it suitable for a barrette or hair comb. When looking at the pieces, make sure to test the idea you are considering by imagining what the end product might be, and then holding it up to the area it is intended for and seeing if the curve makes sense.

When we get to the chapter on *Thinking Caps,* that will be a different matter because the whole cap should sit comfortably on the top of your head. Even though we use the top of a gourd (the leftover part from a gourd bowl) and it's tied on with ribbons, you should test the interior curve to the head for comfort and size. An adult head will not work with the small top of a dipper gourd, and a child's head is just not big enough for the top of a large gourd. But, you will figure all this out as you go along, so let's not get bogged down in details.

Let's get on with the fun!

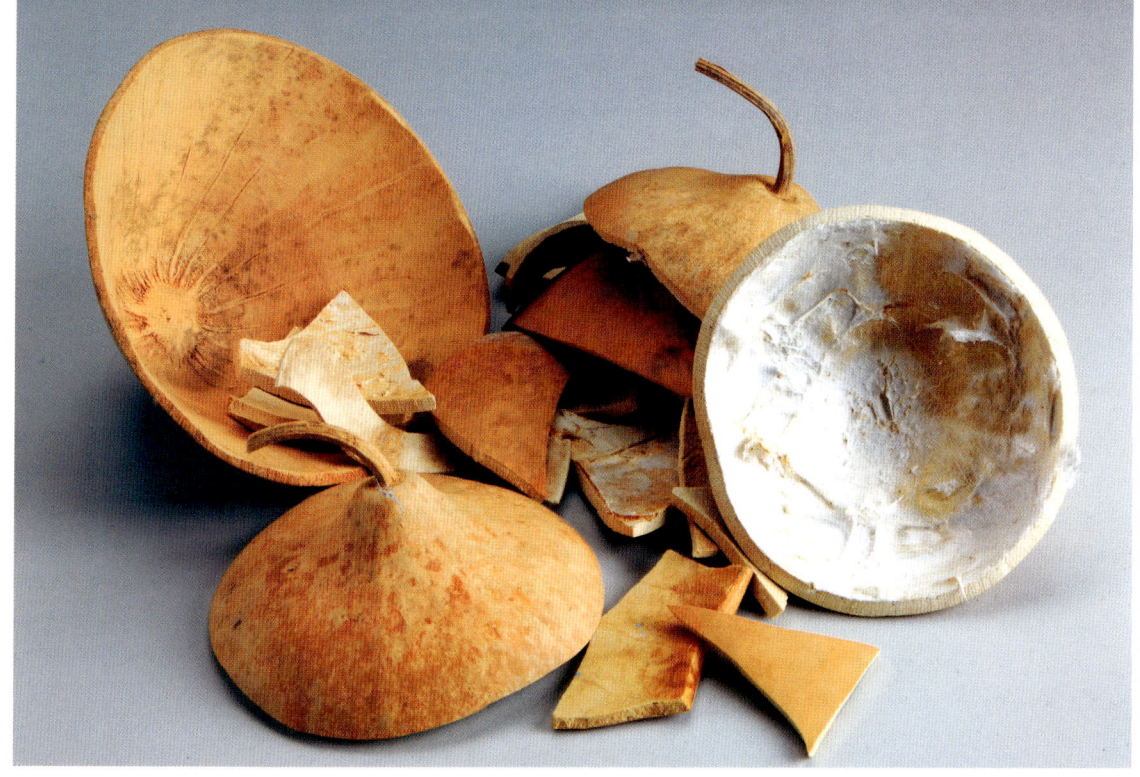

Here is a collection of scraps I have in the garage today, leftover from projects done and gone.

Equipment

I encourage you to use whatever gourd pieces and equipment you already own. I will admit it is tempting to go out to stores or craft shows and buy all sorts of nifty tools and supplies. Many people I admire use wonderful tools of quality and their work shows the level of investment they have made. But, in my garage, the way I see it, I'm working with gourds, nature's freebie, so why not use what I already have on hand? See what you have around the house and test whether or not that works before making any purchases. Then you will know what you really need and what makes sense to buy.

For this book, I did purchase a couple specialty items: the long hatpins, the barrette hardware, and headbands. Everything was found in the craft section of Wal-Mart and a jewelry mail-order catalog, *Fire Mountain Gems,* which is also online. Being as thrifty as I can be, I justify these purchases by saying, 'I'm using up scraps, so it all evens out,' but nothing was pricey. In fact, so inexpensive were the extras, I bought a couple packages of whatever I needed in case I mess up a project or decide to make several versions of a successful concept. After all, when you have a good idea, run with it! (Jewelry suppliers, like Fire Mountain Gems, have so much variety in their inventory, it's hard to stop with only one idea!)

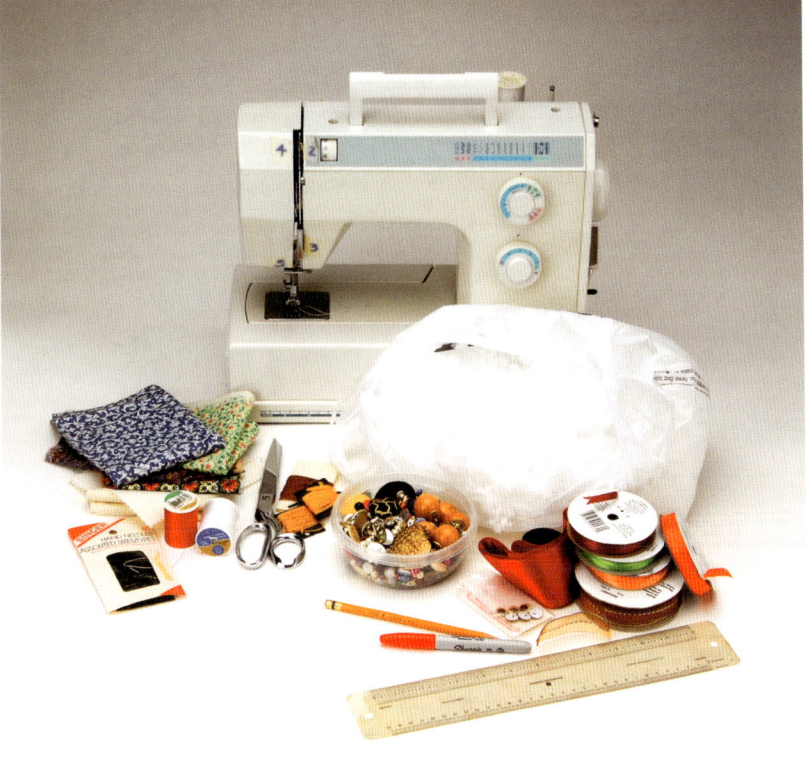

Equipment and tools used for the projects in this book are, from left to right: various pieces of scraps left over from other projects, miniature gourds, jigsaw, drill, wood glue, jewelry hardware, needle and threads, pliers, pencil and permanent markers, spray paints, tapes, decorative craft notions, food coloring, spray varnish, roll of hardware and jewelry wires, headbands and combs, artificial flowers, ribbons, broken pieces of costume jewelry.

Chapter Two:

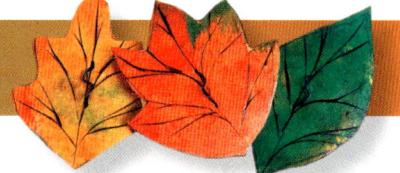

Tiaras

Tiaras are head ornaments intended for occasions when festive or royal duties command extra attention be given to the wearer: birthday, being hostess of the annual neighborhood yard sale, or when the credit card is paid off. A tiara made exclusively of gourd would be beautiful, but only as a decorative item because the first time someone picks it up and tries it on — the sides will snap and break.

But, as we all know, tiaras should be worn! The tiaras here are basically pieces of gourd attached to a headband or a comb, then decorated with beads and wire. No two are alike, nor can they be, due to different gourd shapes and sizes. Therefore, we will look at a couple techniques that will most likely lead you to many ideas of your own.

Let's move ahead, royally speaking.

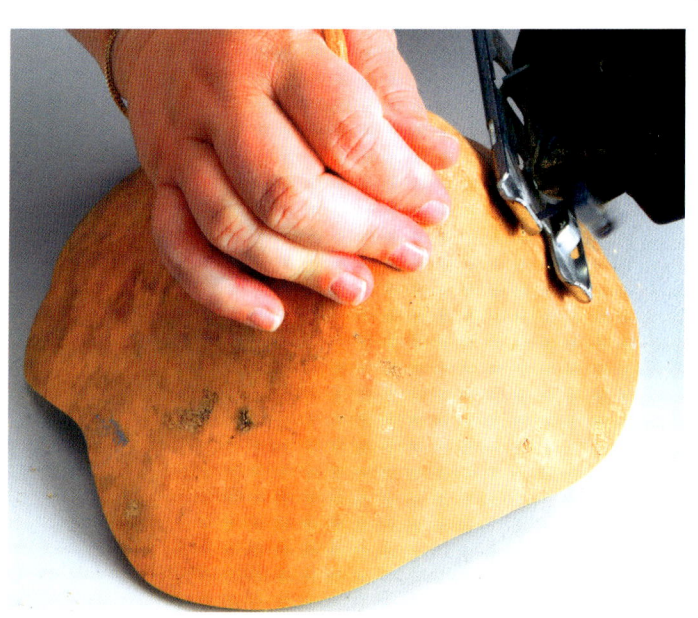

Here is the top half of a kettle gourd that was cut for a bowl. Using a jigsaw, cut a line around the gourd about 3-4" from the edge to release a ring of gourd.

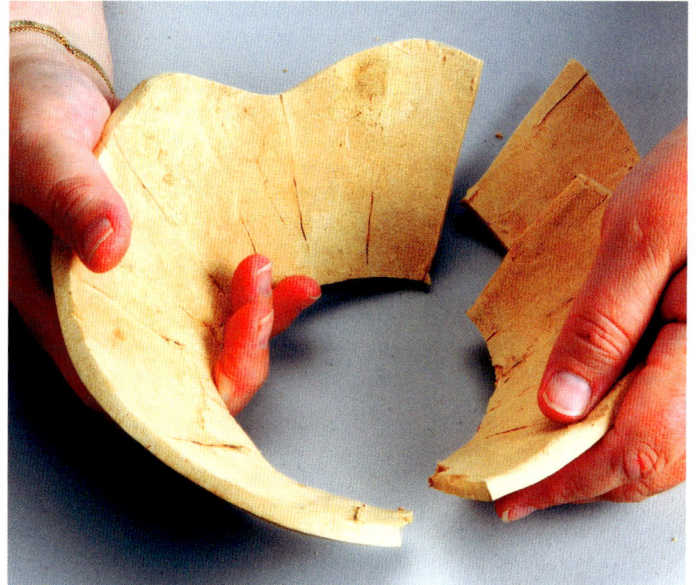

Holding the ring, compress it enough to snap it in half.

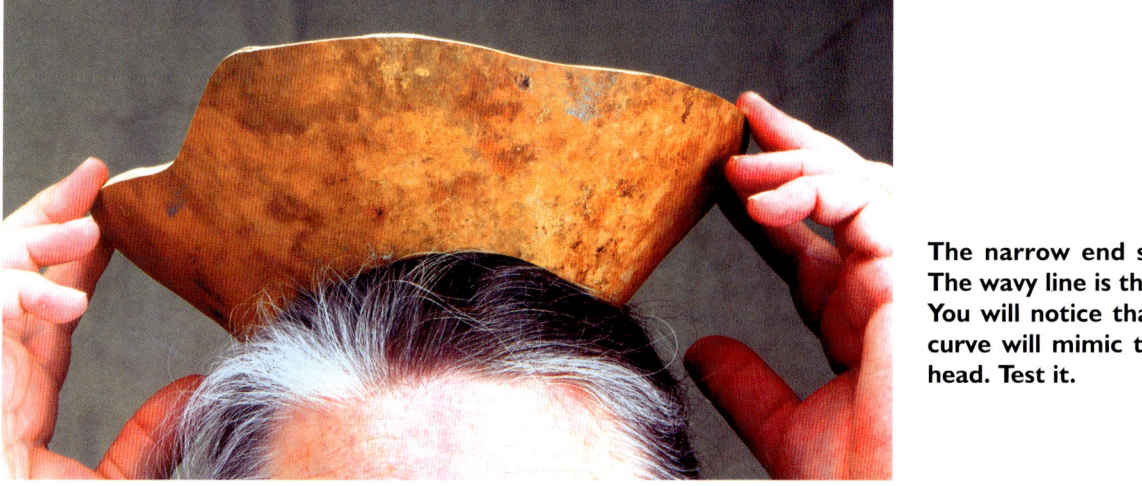

The narrow end sits against the head. The wavy line is the top line of the tiara. You will notice that the gourd's natural curve will mimic the natural curve of a head. Test it.

8

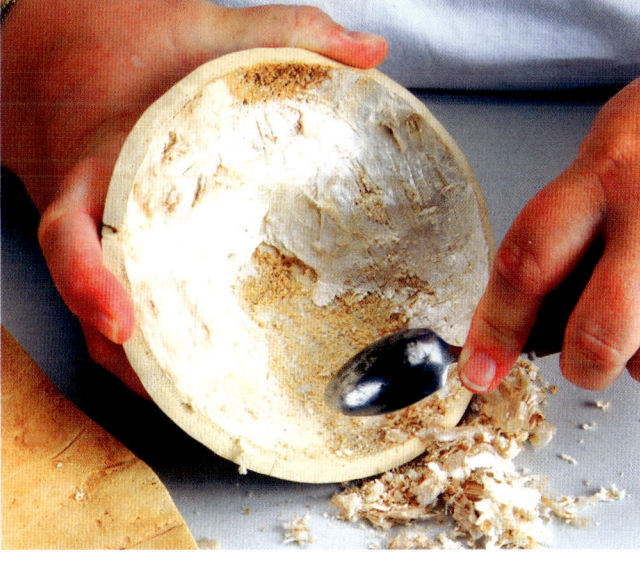

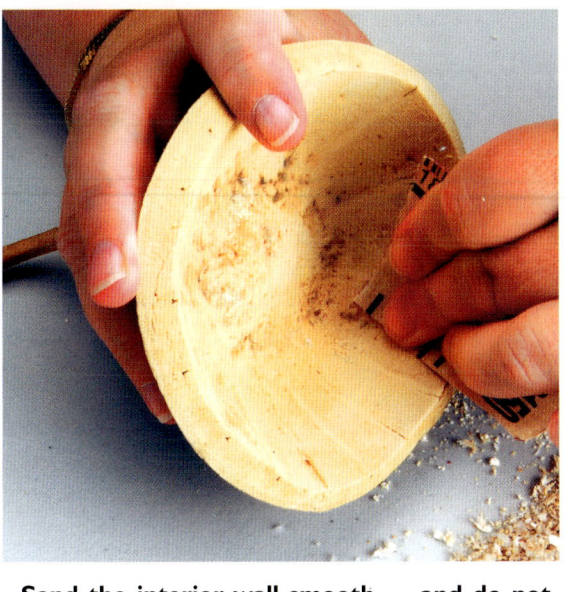

This particular piece had been gutted at one time; if yours has not, scrape away any pith leftover from the dehydrating process.

Sand the interior wall smooth — and do not forget to wear a mask!

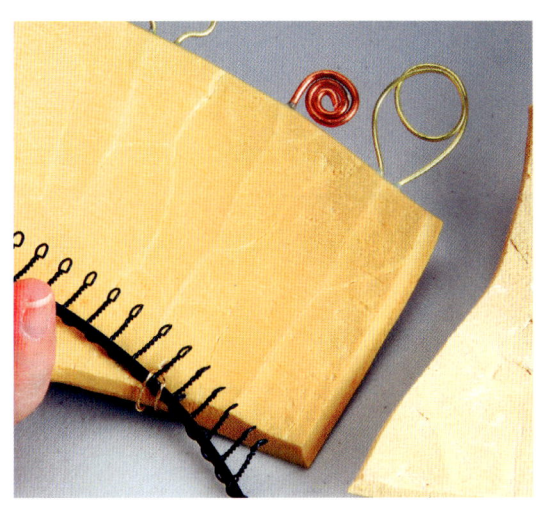

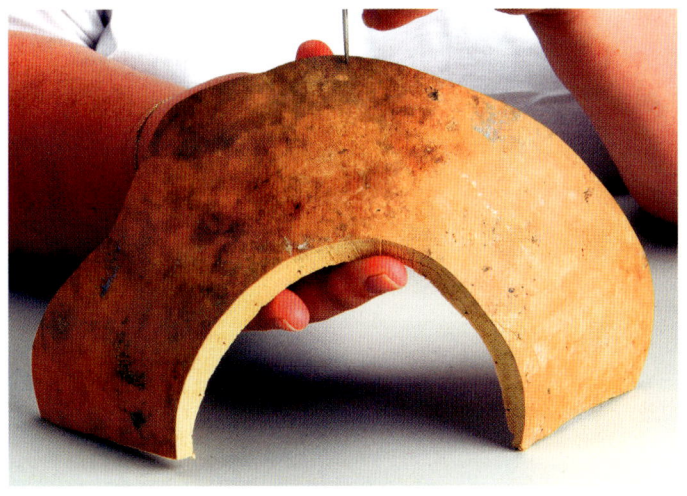

The level of finishing is your personal choice. The tiara I wear at the Virginia Gourd Festival is finished with a finer hand than the one I made for the garage.

Find the center of your tiara, and mark it with a hole at the crown with a darning needle. This will be the center of the tiara and will help you judge space as you work from one side to the other.

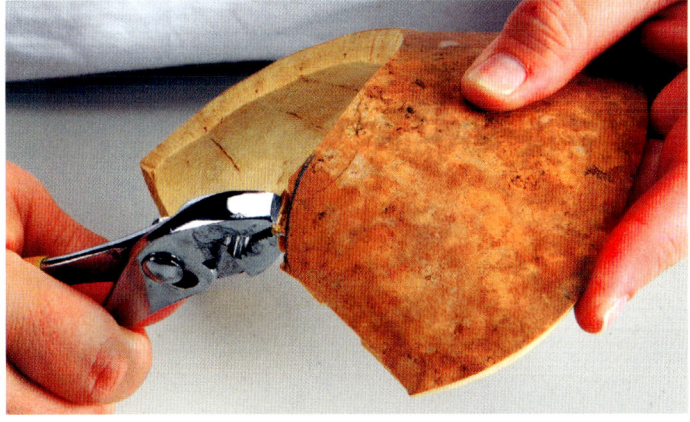

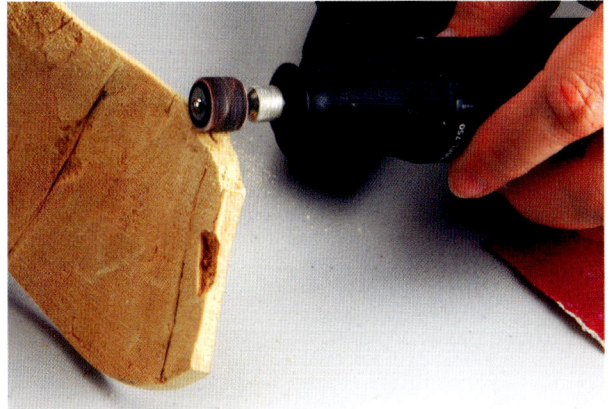

Use pliers to pinch a curved edge to the bottom corners of the tiara. Take small pinches, don't overpinch.

Sand the curved edges until they're smooth. I sand against a vacuum nozzle. Mask...remember to wear the mask!

9

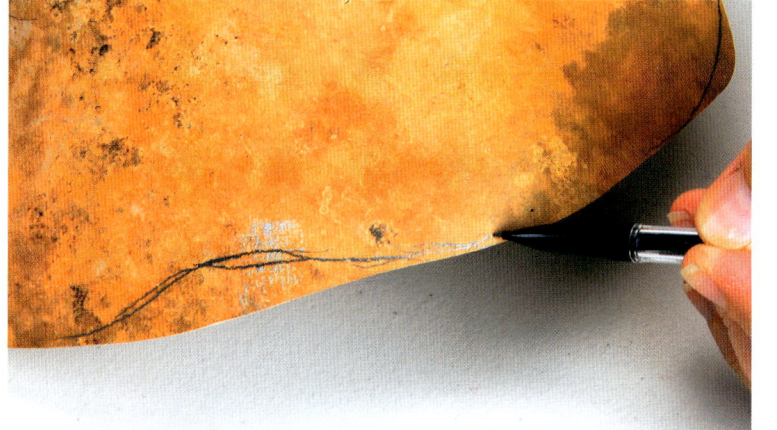

To create an interesting top edge, pencil the line you prefer. Not too detailed.

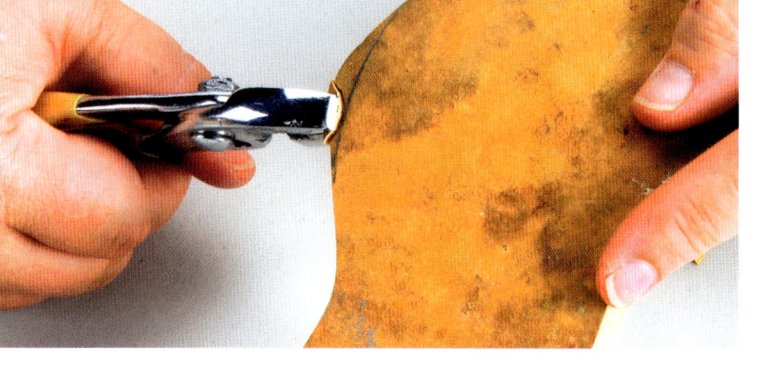

Using needle-nosed or regular pliers, take small pinches on the edge of the gourd and break off small pieces.

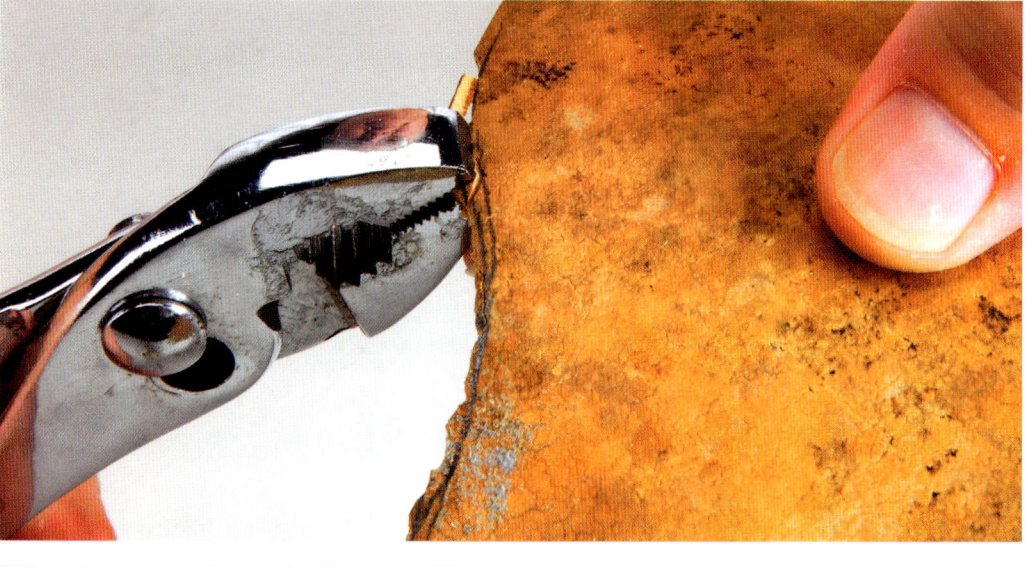

Do not attempt large pieces unless you want to dismiss a large corner because the larger the piece you try to take, the more random the break line. You want the gourd to pinch off where **YOU** want it to pinch.

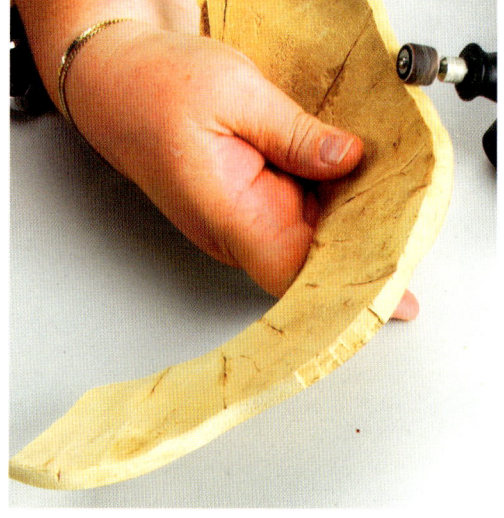

Once the top line is established, sand the jagged edges. I am using a Dremel with a sanding bit.

We will be drilling decorative holes across the top edge of the tiara. Find a scrap piece of wood or other material that you won't mind getting marred with a drill hole. This will serve as a drilling base.

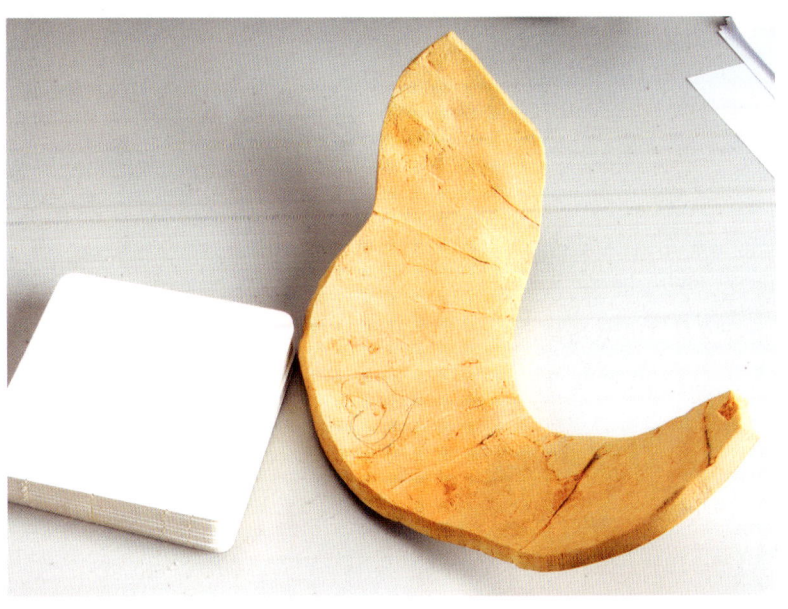

Insert a 7/8" drill bit, in order to drill two 7/8" holes, side-by-side.

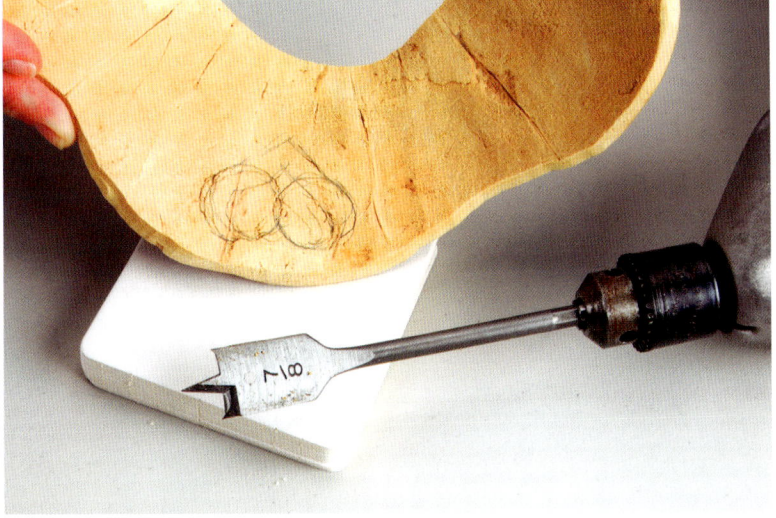

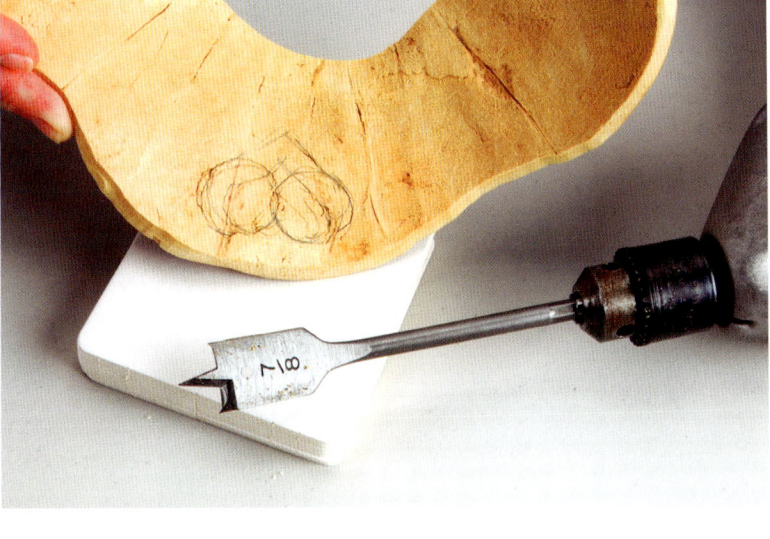

Working from the backside, place the drilling area on the base. Put the center of the 7/8" bit in one of the circles, and drill. Drill two holes side-by-side to form the top of a heart-shaped opening.

Using a coping saw blade clamped in the jaws of a locking wrench, cut lines from the outside of the holes to a center point under the holes to finish forming the heart-shaped opening.

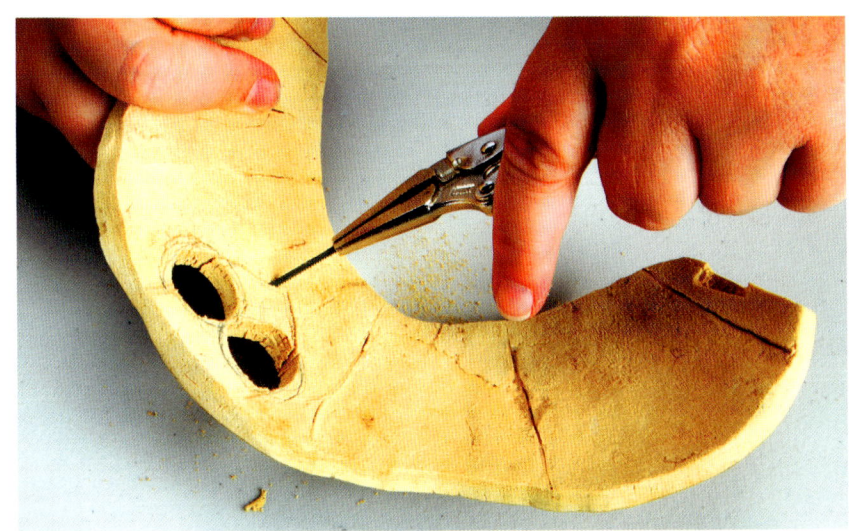

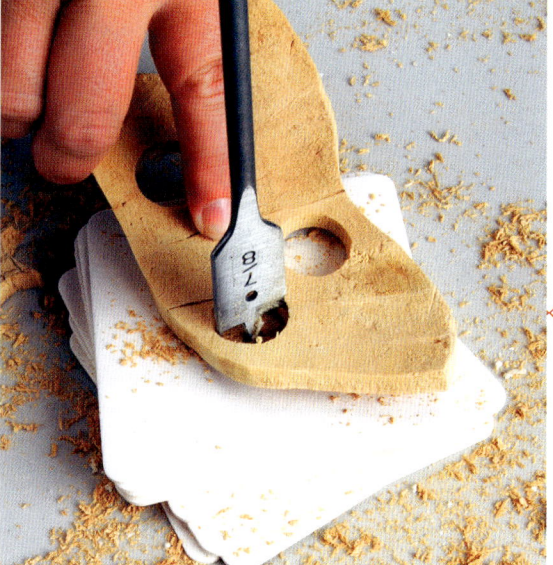

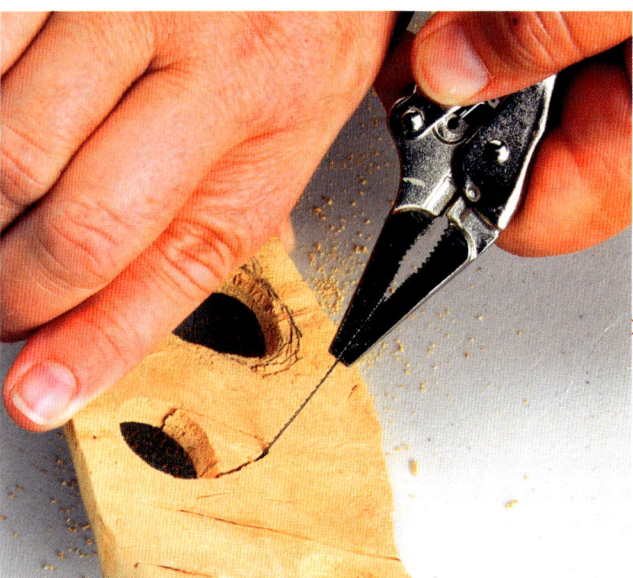

Drilling holes will also work for making drops. Just use the same technique of drilling the initial hole...

...then cutting down from either side of the hole to a center point below the hole.

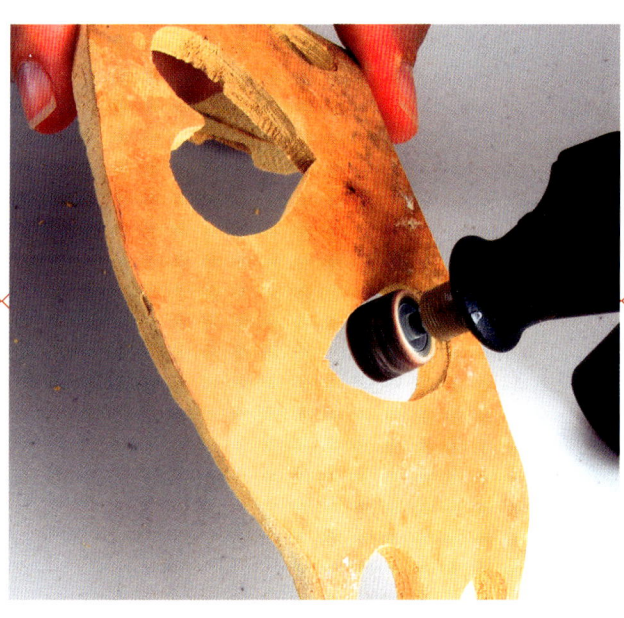

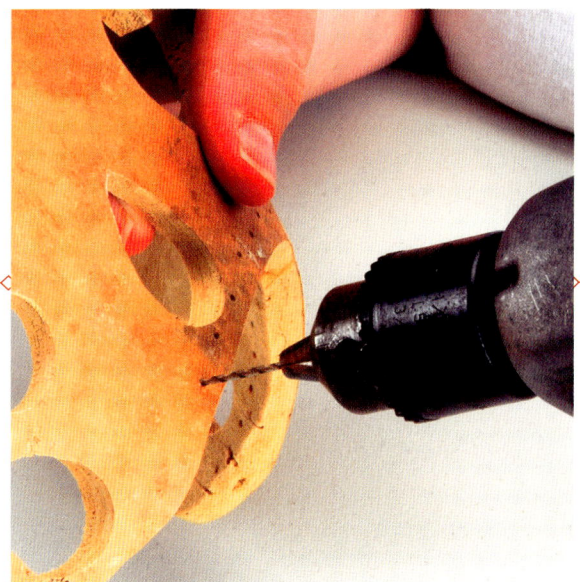

Sand the interior of the openings.

Once you have the main tiara holes and perforations done, use a 1/16" drill bit and make a series of holes about ½" apart along the bottom edge of the tiara. These will be the holes to use when attaching a headband.

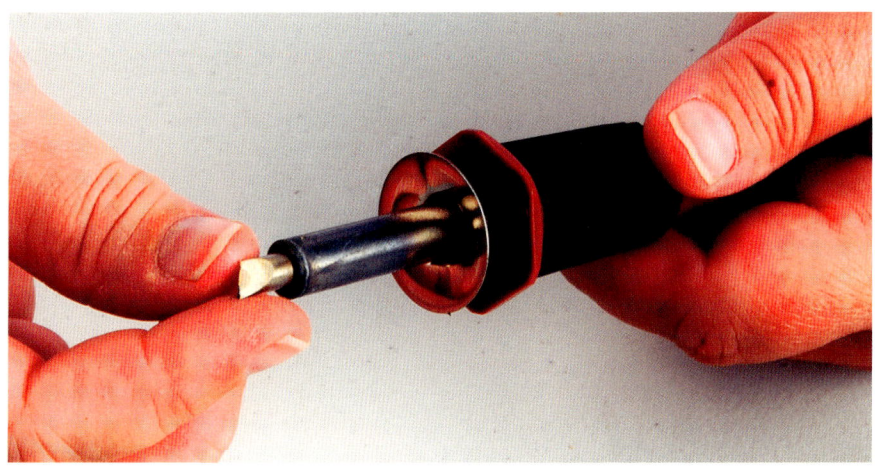

For detailing decoration on the tiara, screw a chisel point into the woodburner...

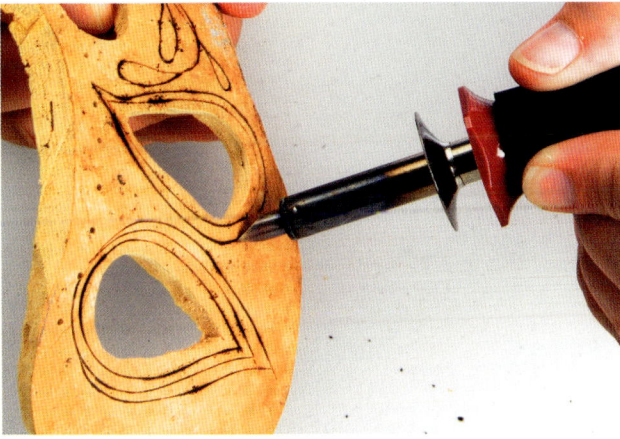

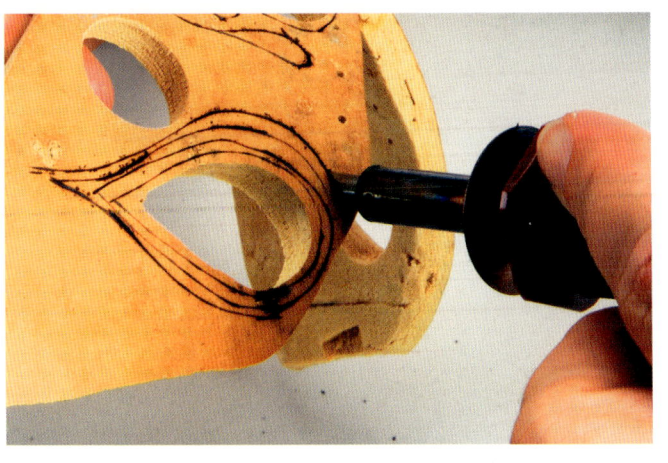

...and burn lines on the front surface of the gourd tiara that mimic the holes and edges you have already made.

These lines can use a technique called 'shadowing,' where an initial line is made and all the following lines shadow the previous line.

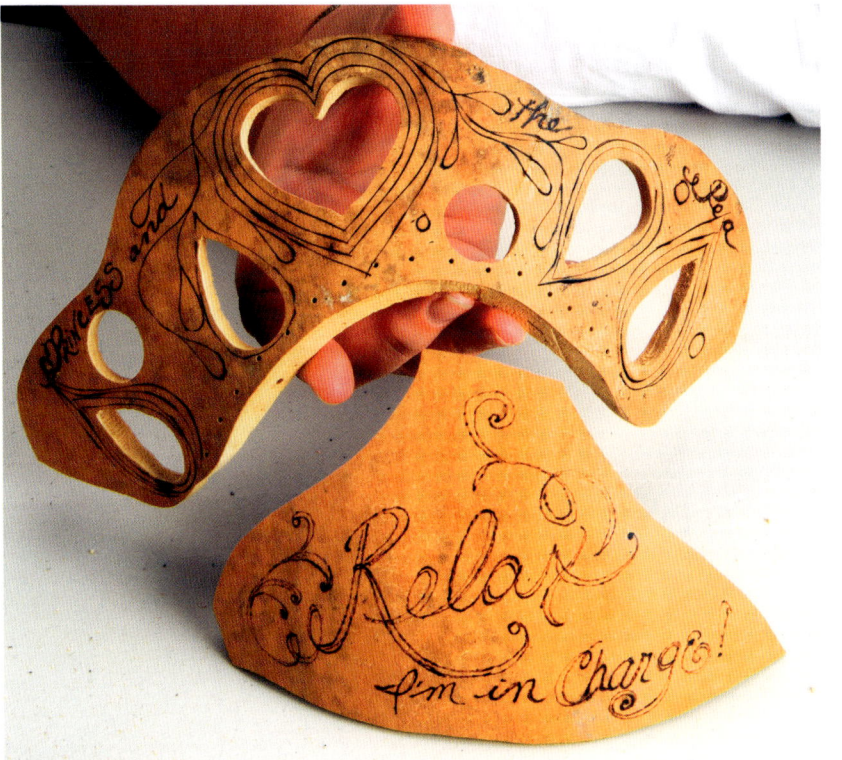

Words and images can be added for personal touches. I use a woodburner a lot because then the line becomes a permanent part of the gourd and imparts a little texture. Here are examples of words in the design and another where the words are the design.

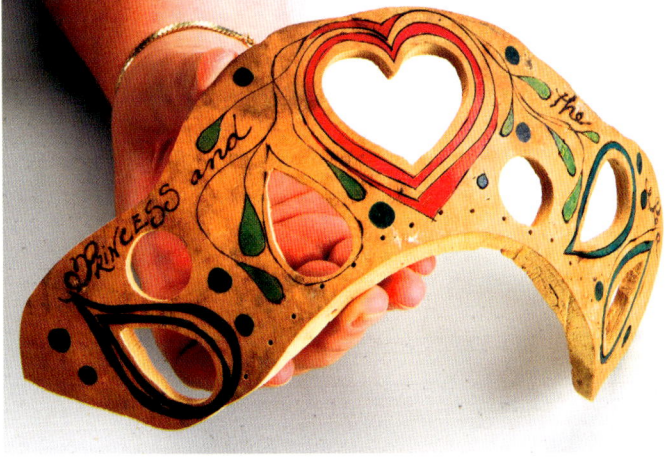

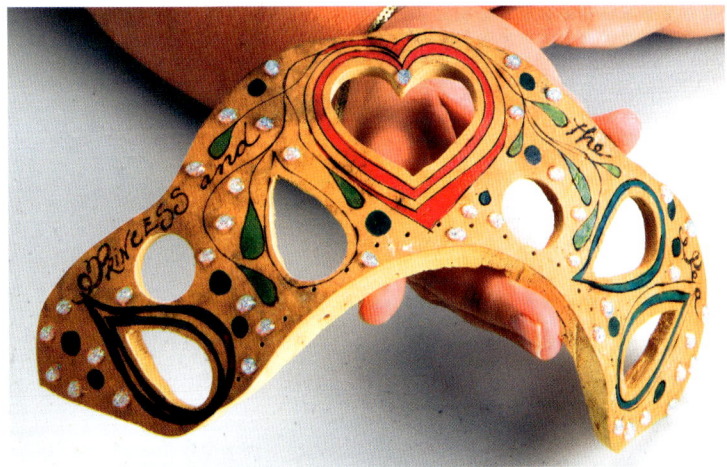

After lines or art have been added, color with paints or permanent markers.

Use glitter glue for dots or lines of sparkle.

13

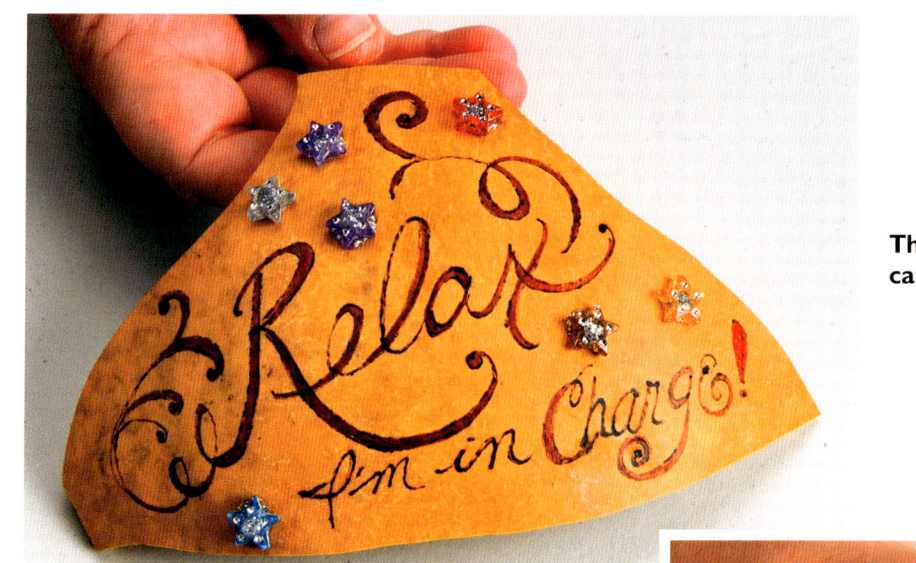

The addition of gems are a nice touch as you can see from this particular tiara.

Sometimes an added piece of costume jewelry gives just the right touch!

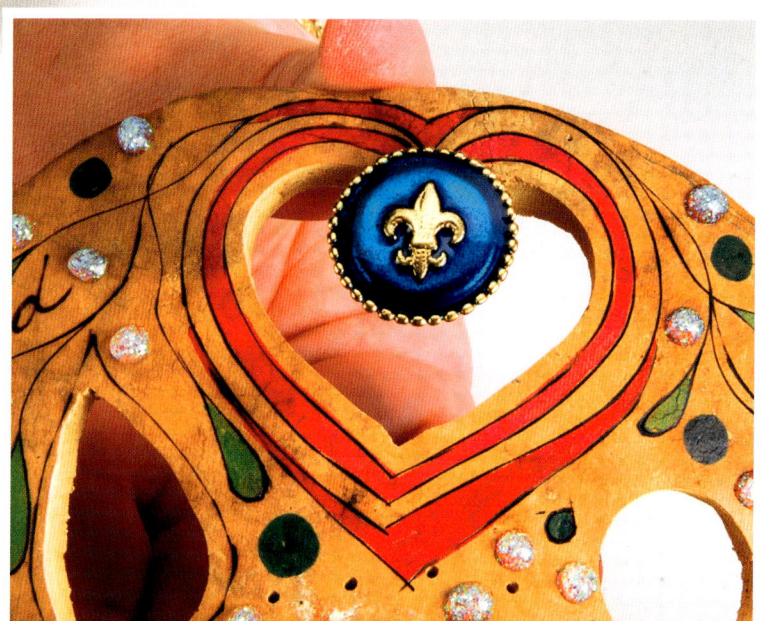

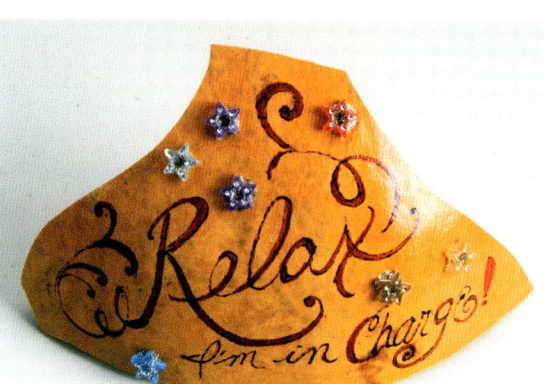

After the color is applied and you feel happy with the design, spray or brush on several layers of lacquer or varnish. Make sure to use thin layers so any colors from permanent markers do not bleed. Dry thoroughly between layers.

While our tiara is drying, let's add some danglies to the other tiara we designed.

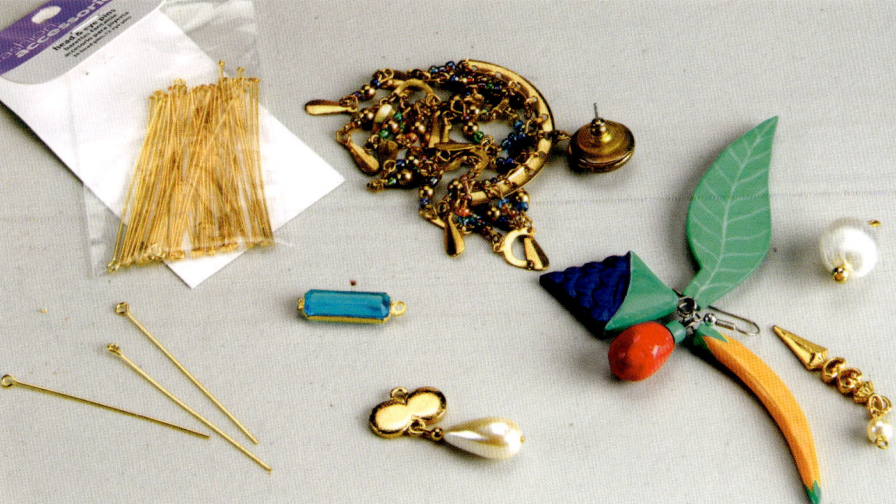 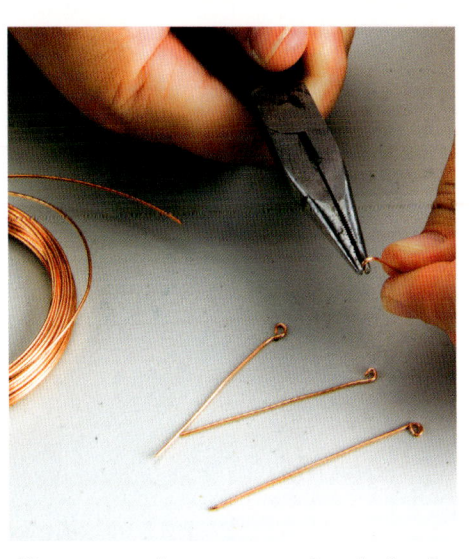

These are pieces of costume jewelry and head-pins. Head-pins are used to hang the jewelry.

You can make your own head-pins by using pieces of wire and needle-nosed pliers to turn tight hooks on one end.

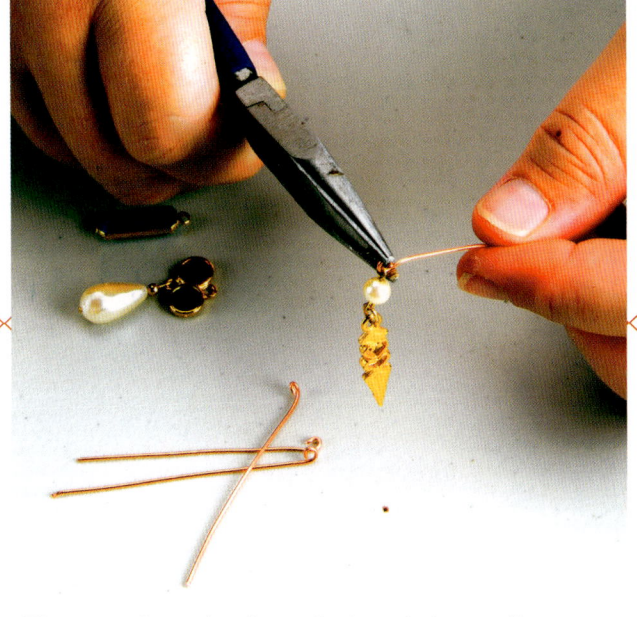 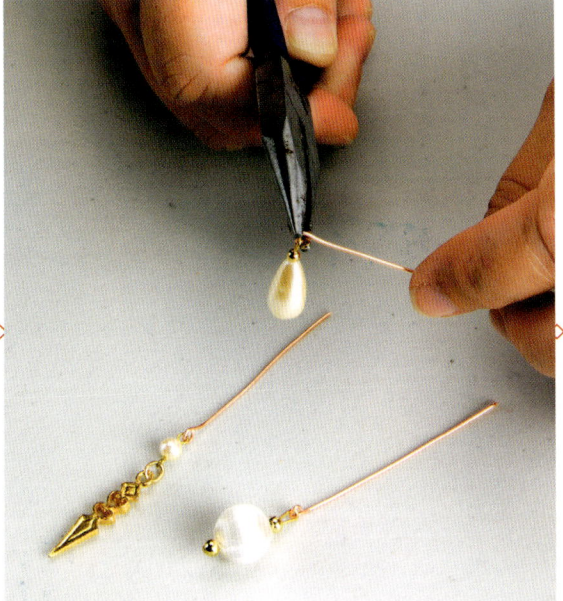

The curved part is where the bangle hangs. Squeeze the hook shut so that the bangle is secure.

Back to the tiara with danglies: select three pieces of costume jewelry and hang them from your head-pins.

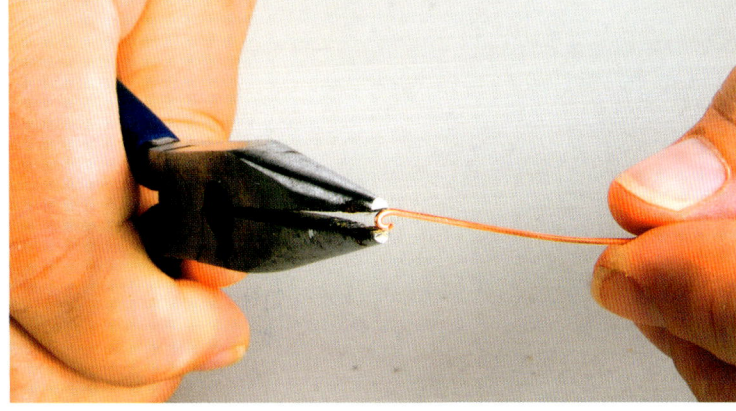 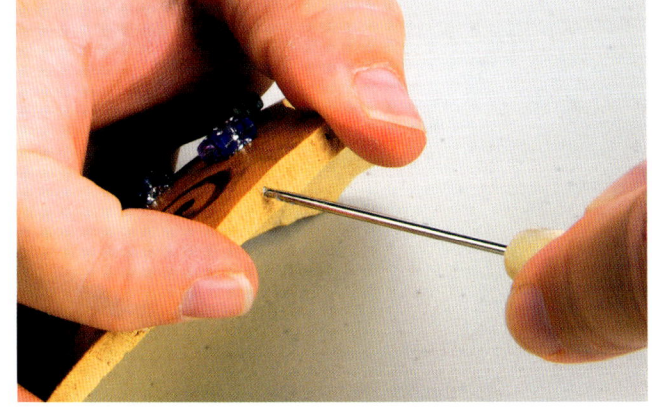

At the opposite end of the head-pin, make a tiny, collapsed hook.

Using a darning needle, make holes along the top edge of the tiara that are about ¼" deep. Start with a center hole...

15

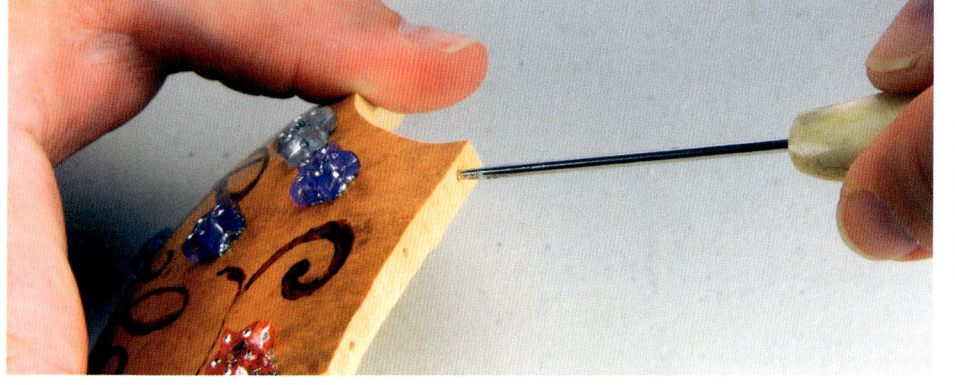

...then continue with holes on either side of center. Note: Choose an odd number of danglies for your tiaras, so that one will be the center and the others fan away from center in an equidistant fashion.

Once the holes are made, squeeze a small amount of wood glue into the holes.

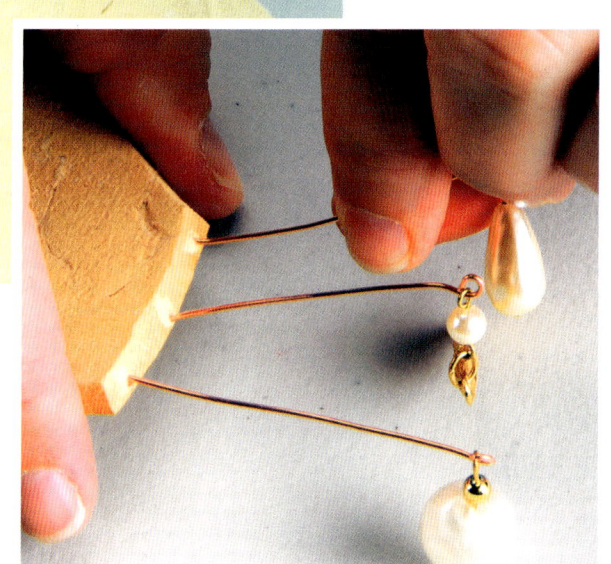

Insert the collapsed end of the headpins into the holes. The small hook acts as a grabbing device that gets tangled with the dried glue to anchor the headpins in place.

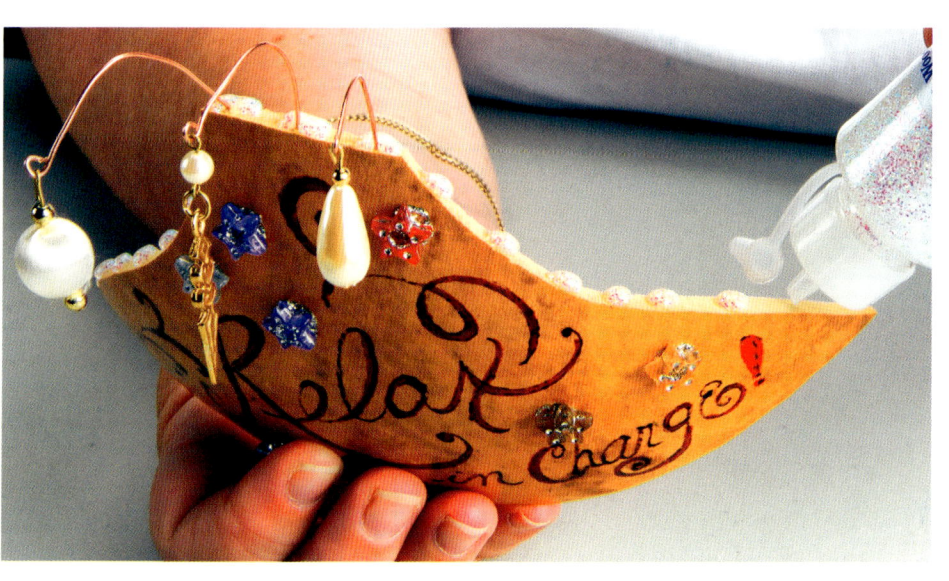

After the glue has dried, bend the wires forward a little so that the danglies can move freely when the wearer walks. This is the time to add any additional glitter-glue to the rim of the tiara.

16

Full Wrap

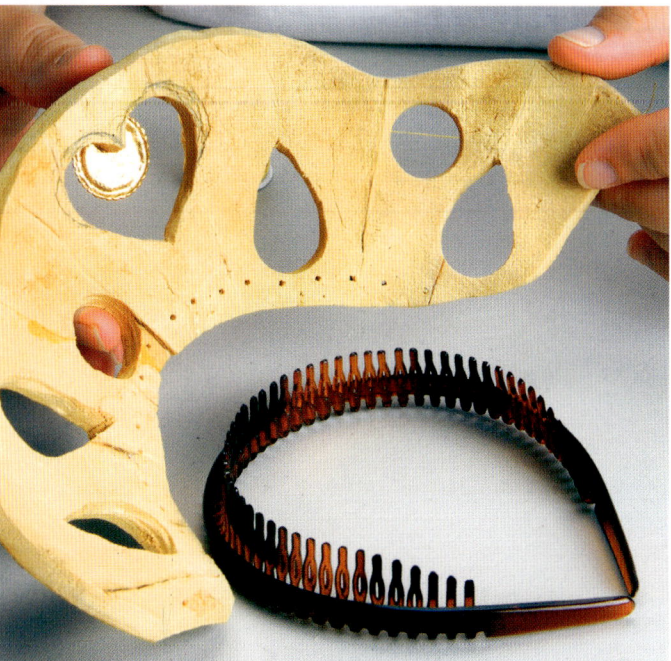

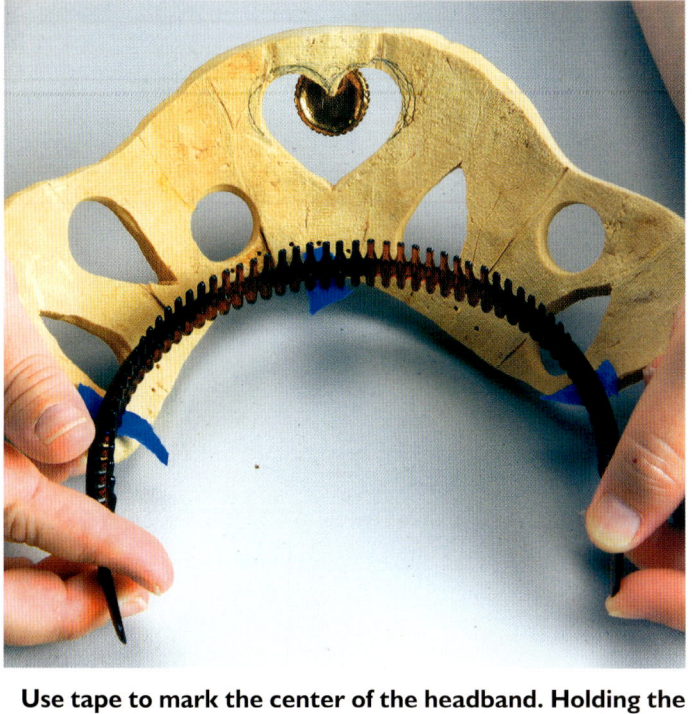

To make a tiara practical, and wearable on a daily basis, it has to be attached to a headband. Our original tiara, now dry, has 1/16" holes drilled across the bottom edge. These will be used in connecting the headband to the tiara.

Use tape to mark the center of the headband. Holding the headband against the tiara will show where the tiara ends on the headband. Mark the ending places on the headband with tape.

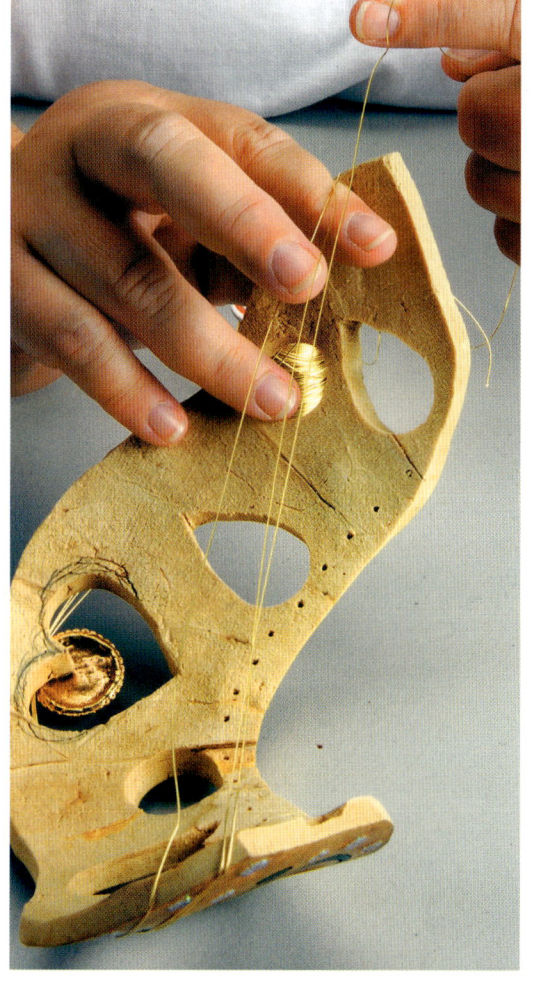

To measure enough wire to connect the tiara to the headband, use the tiara itself as a measuring device. The amount of wire you will probably need encircles the tiara three times. I spiral the wire around the tiara as if I am spooling yarn.

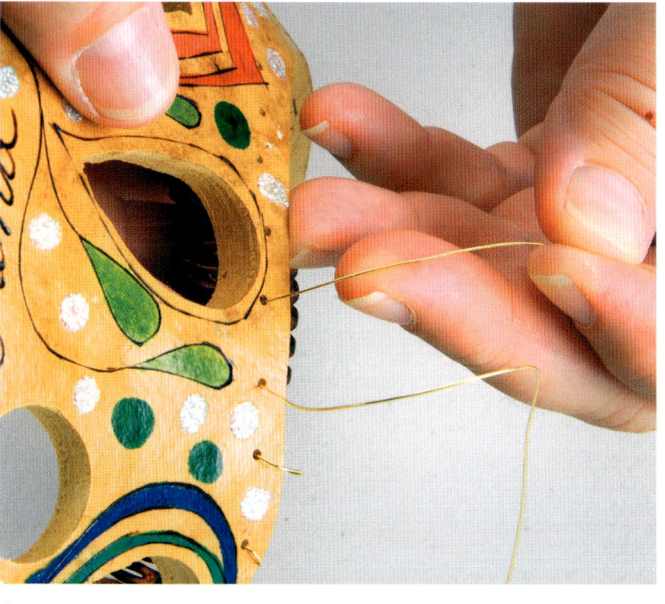

Start at one side of the headband, wrapping the wire around the headband and through the holes at the bottom of the tiara. I am using 26-gauge brass wire to do this.

17

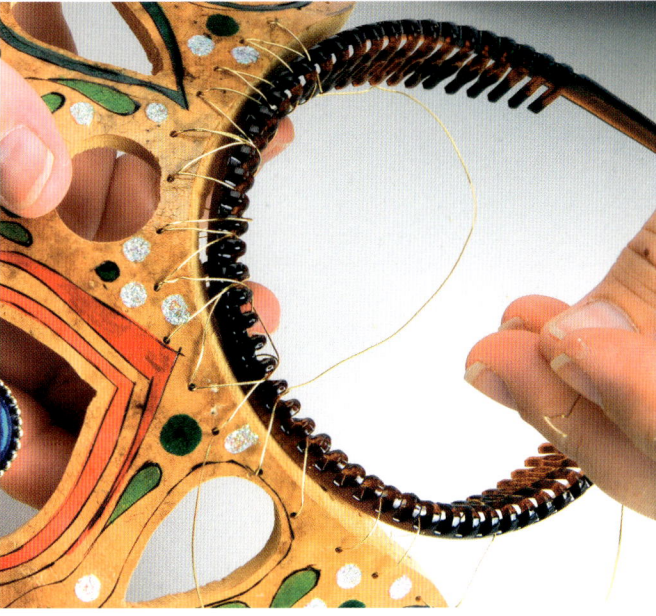
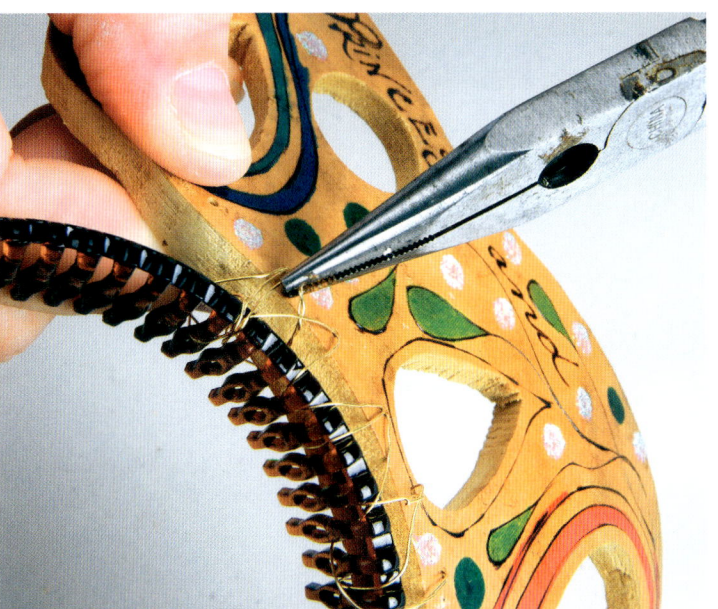

Continue this sewing technique across the bottom edge of the tiara, and then turn and go back.

When you return to the starting point, twist the wire's ends together, trim, and then tuck the ends out of the way.

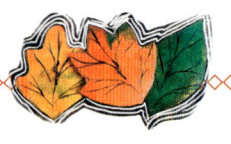

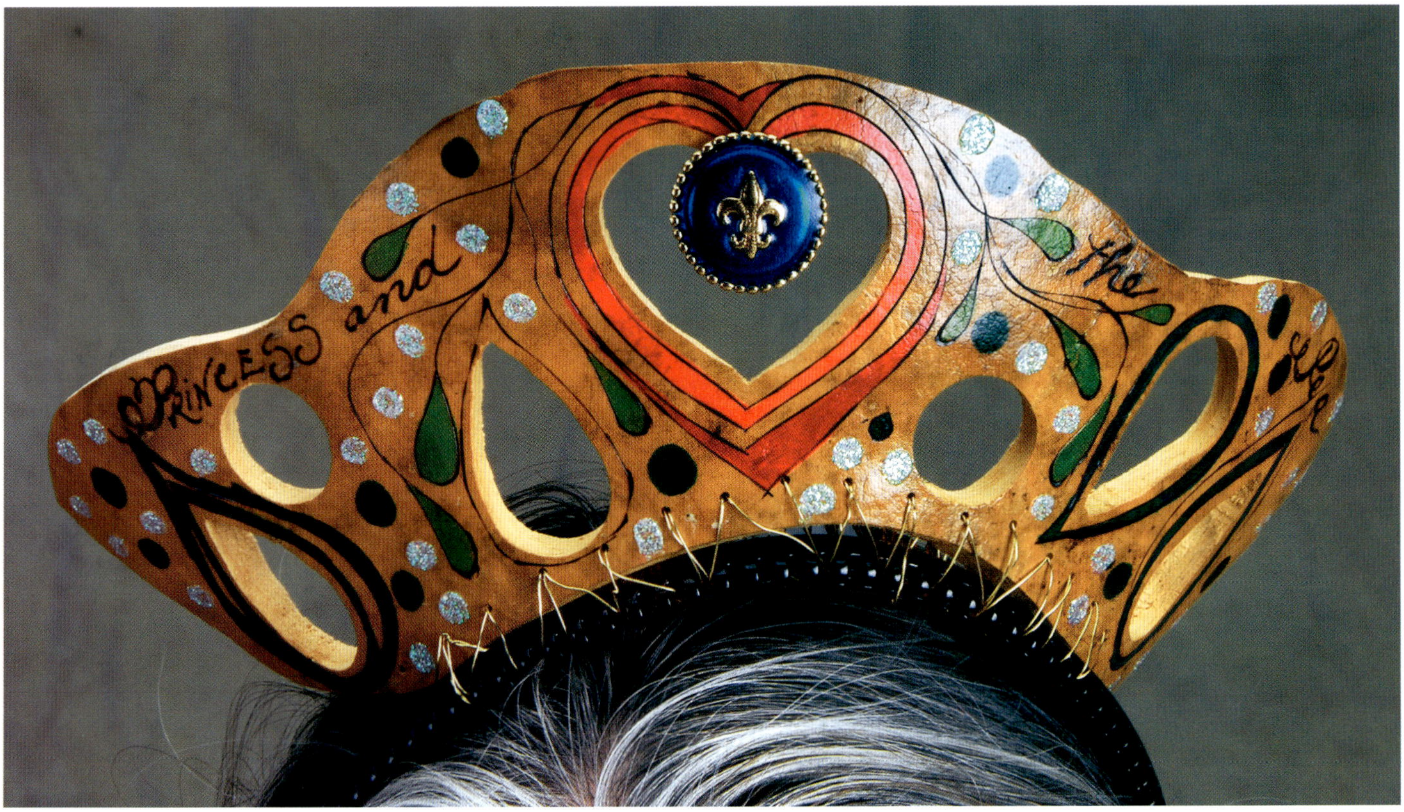

Ta-Da!!

Comb

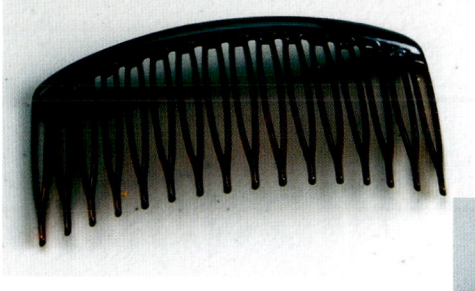

To make a smaller tiara, a princess tiara to the queen tiara, use a hair comb as the base.

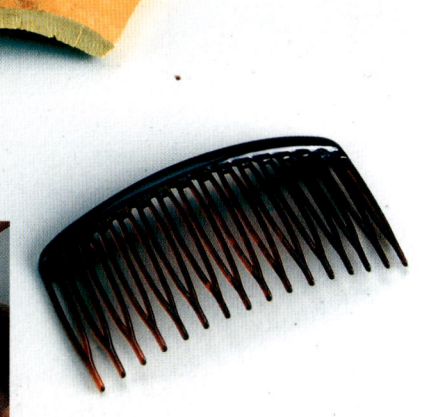

Select a scrap from the ring that we compressed earlier. It should have a flat bottom edge, so that it can sit flat against the head.

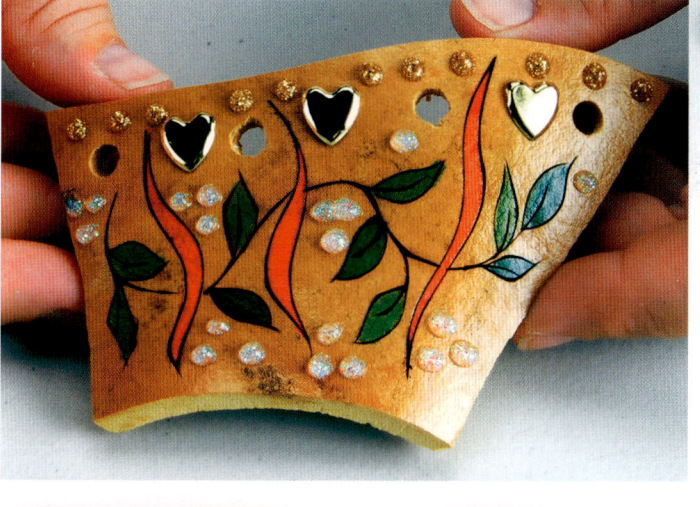

Decorate it as you please.

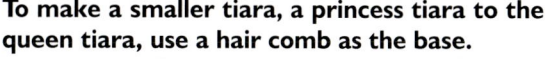

Drill only five holes along the bottom edge of the gourd scrap, toward the center.

19

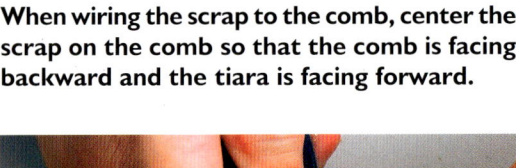

When wiring the scrap to the comb, center the scrap on the comb so that the comb is facing backward and the tiara is facing forward.

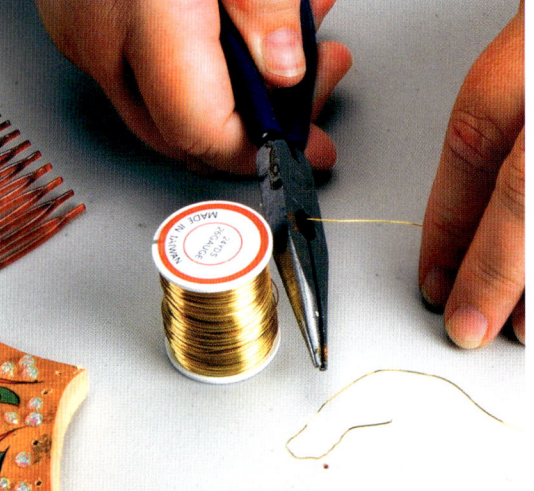

Cut a piece of jewelry wire 18" long.

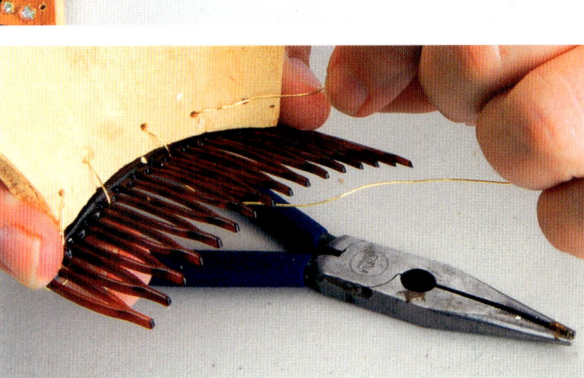

Wire the tiara in the perpendicular position shown earlier, so it will stand up from the head when worn. Wire from one side to the other, and back again. Make sure that you wire perpendicular to the comb, and not tilting back.

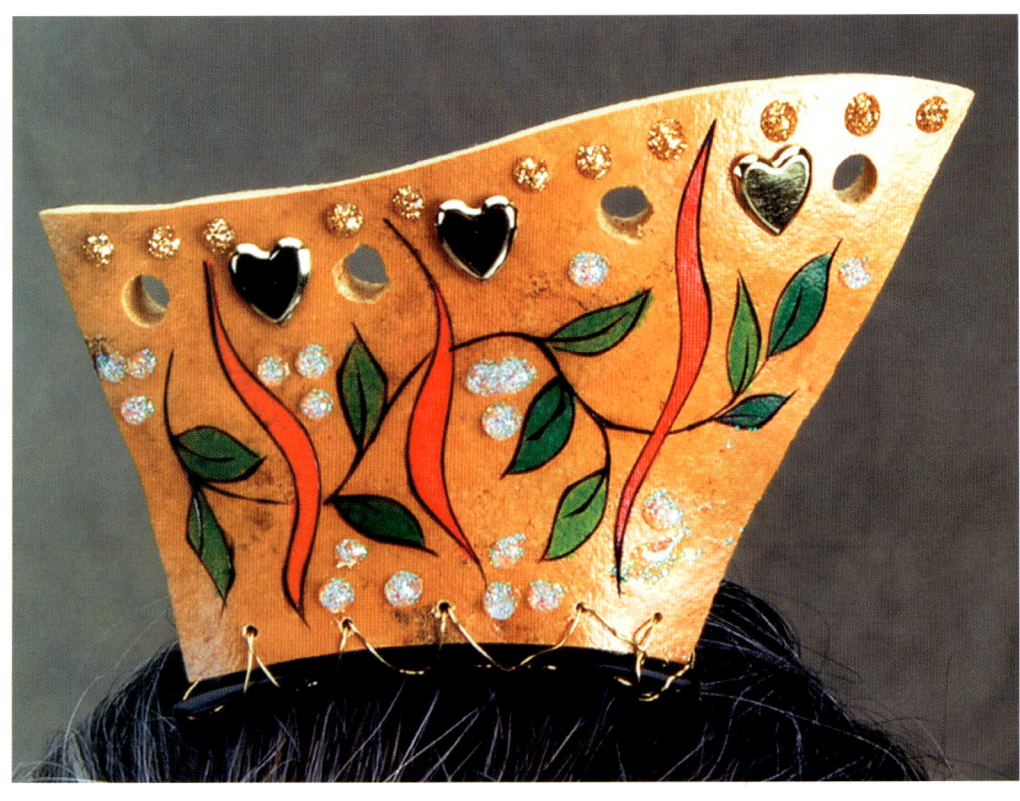

Voilá!

20

Chapter Three:

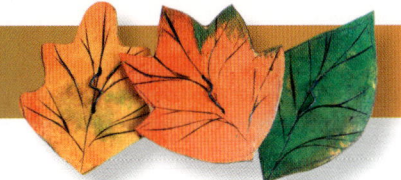

Harvest Heads

Harvest time is a natural season for gourds. The fields are full of the wonders of the season's bounty while the trees display the colors of warm autumn days. Whether it's an autumn wedding, a harvest festival, or a Thanksgiving holiday, nothing beats the festive look of combining small, well-shaped gourds with multi-colored leaves and ribbon. We are using mini-bottleneck gourds in the following projects. In fact, when I come across an especially small gourd in the garden, I make sure I put it aside for these types of projects.

Let's band together some gourds!

Headband

To make a headband, choose an inexpensive headband from a local shop.

Select an odd number of mini-gourds, autumn leaves or flowers with stems, and a piece of satin ribbon that is three times wider and six inches longer than the headband.

21

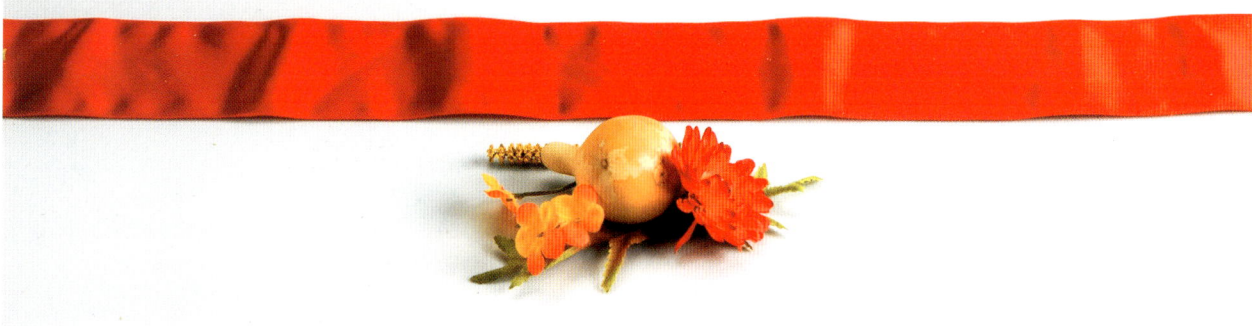

Lay the ribbon on the table and line up the items in a pleasing manner by starting at the center and working toward the sides.

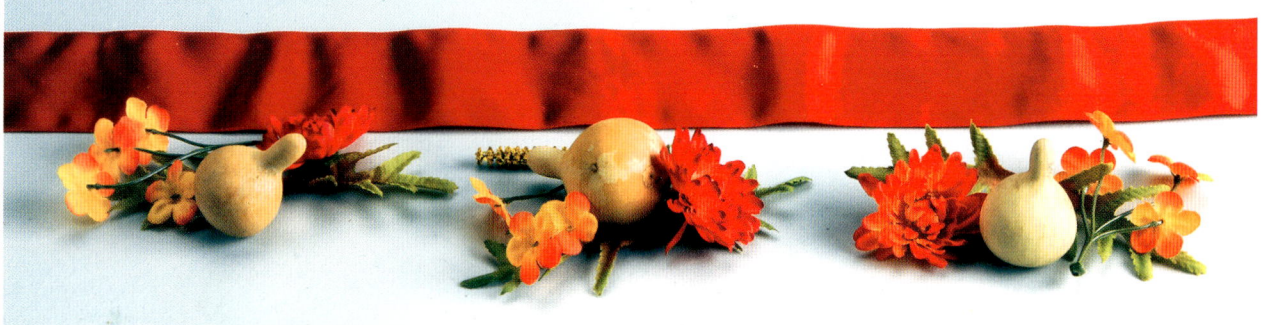

Add to one side and then add to the other side, until a balance is achieved.

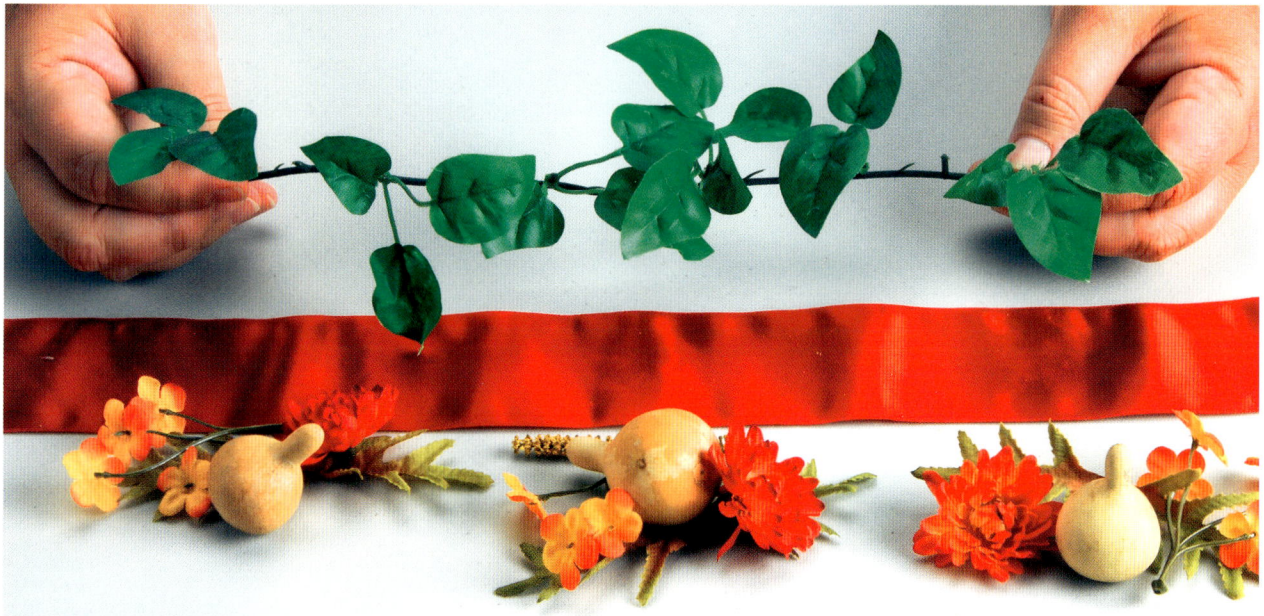

Use a section of artificial vine as the common thread between the three sets or groupings of gourds, leaves, and flowers you arranged earlier.

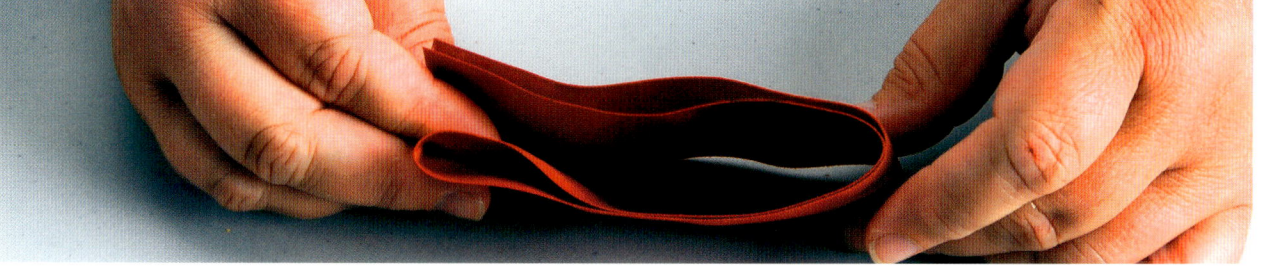

Fold the ribbon in half, and in half again.

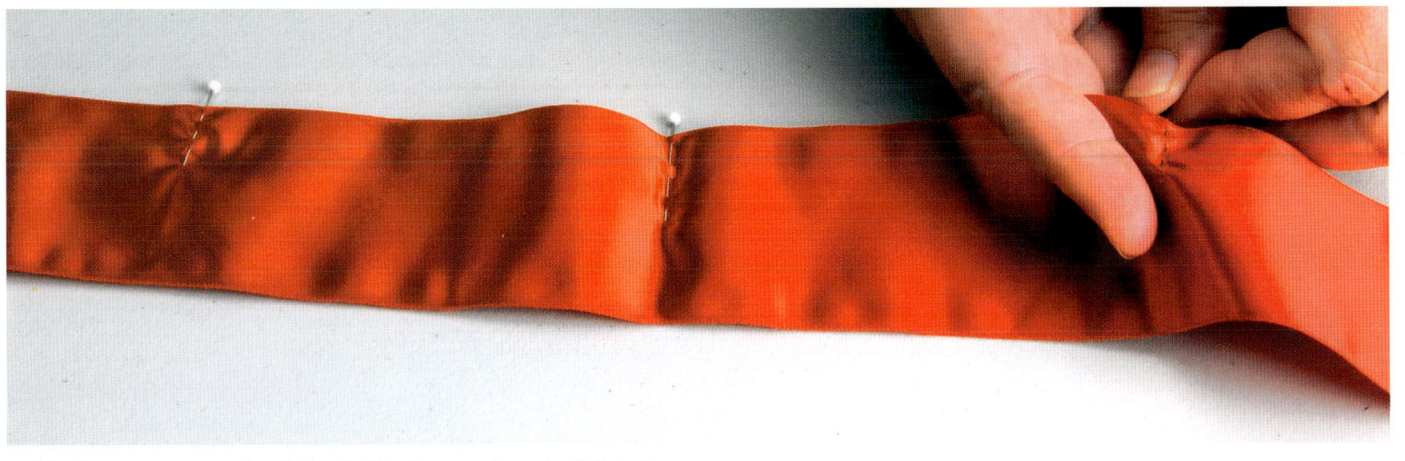

Mark a spot at each of the folds. I am using straight pins.

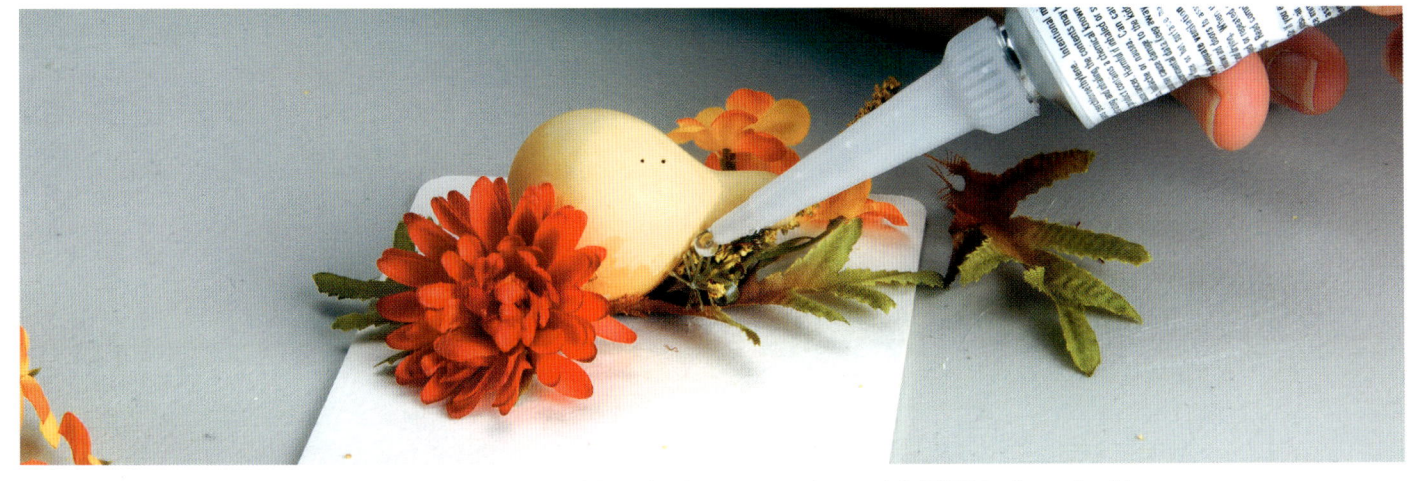

The gourds and leaves will be bonded to the ribbon in three groupings with E6000 glue; the biggest pieces are generally centered, with smaller pieces to the sides. *(Note: Hot glue will soften in the hot sun, so a bonding glue such as E6000 is best.)*

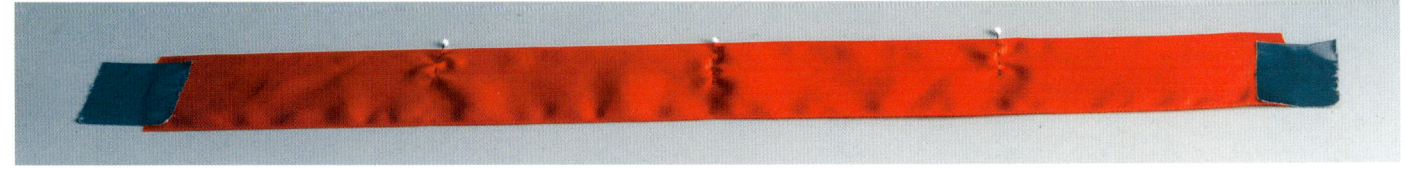

Tape the ribbon's ends to the table, to keep them from moving.

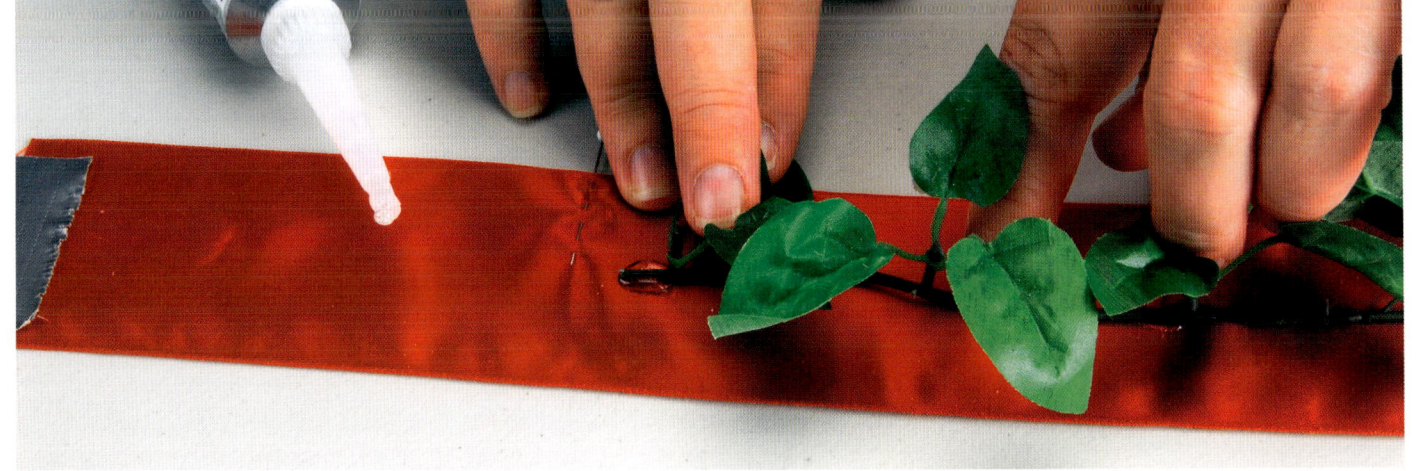

Center the vine over the three pins, and bond it to the ribbon with dots of E6000 glue.

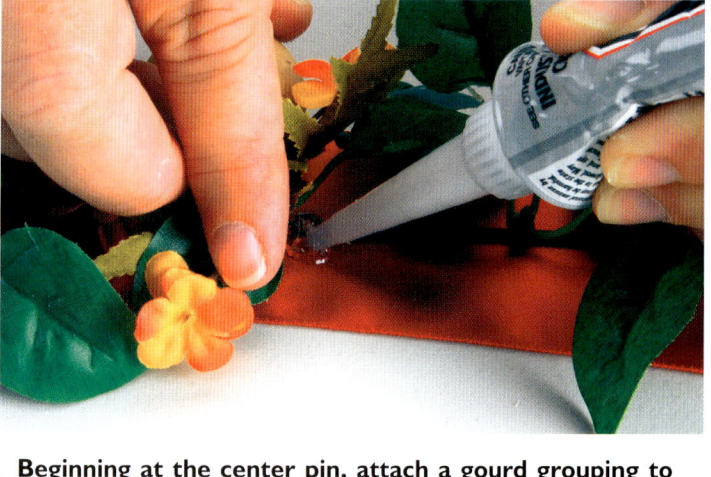 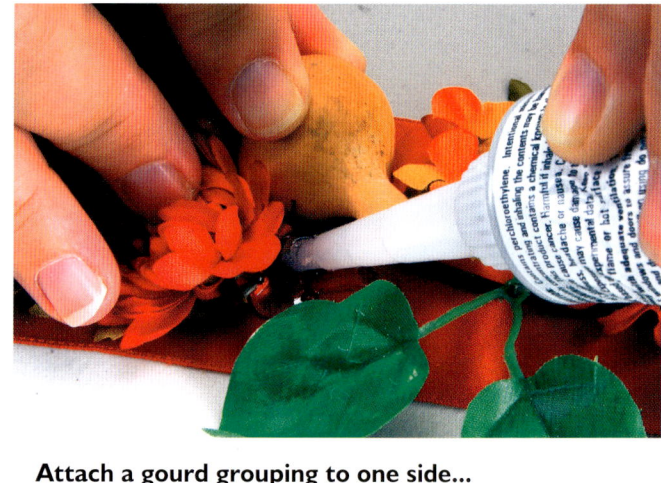

Beginning at the center pin, attach a gourd grouping to the vine and ribbon with dabs of E6000 glue.

Attach a gourd grouping to one side...

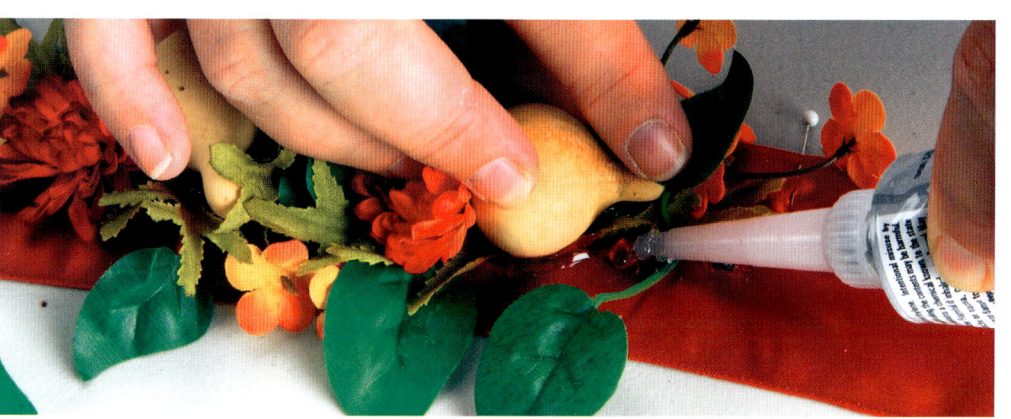

...and then the other.

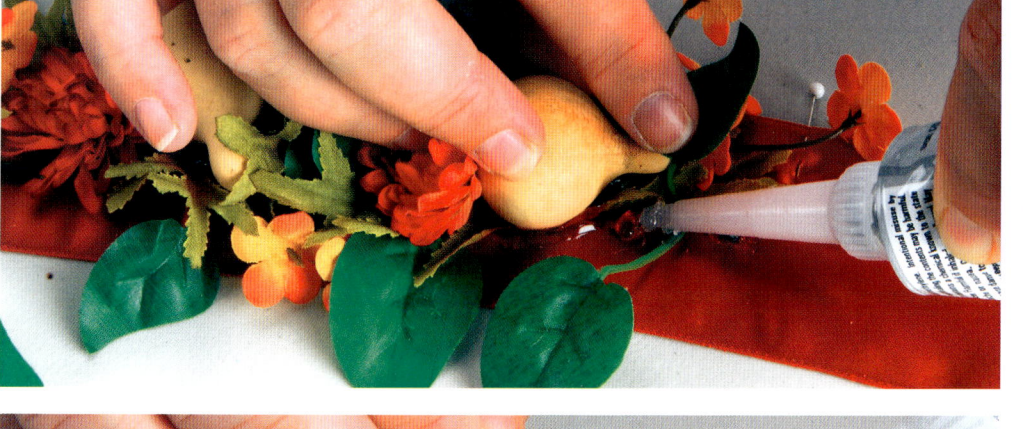

Place two extra gourds between the center and side gourd groupings.

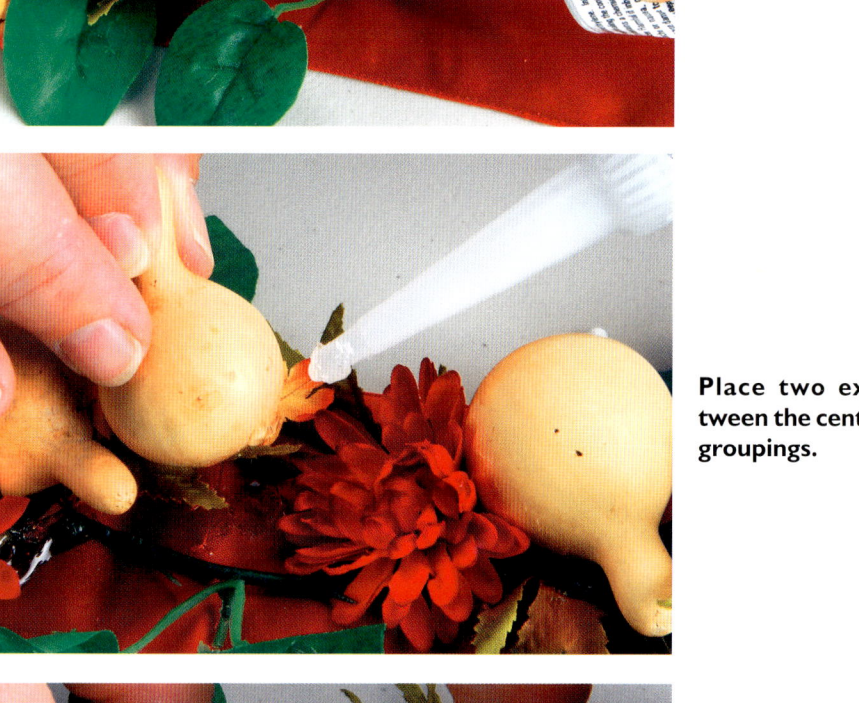

Leaves can be added as filler for any hollow spaces.

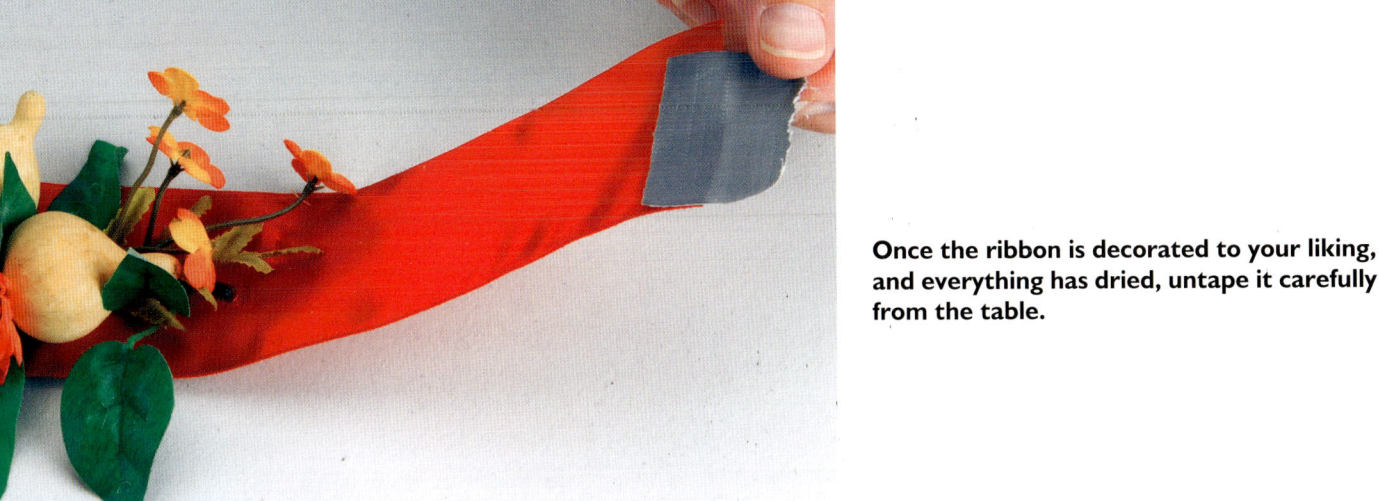

Once the ribbon is decorated to your liking, and everything has dried, untape it carefully from the table.

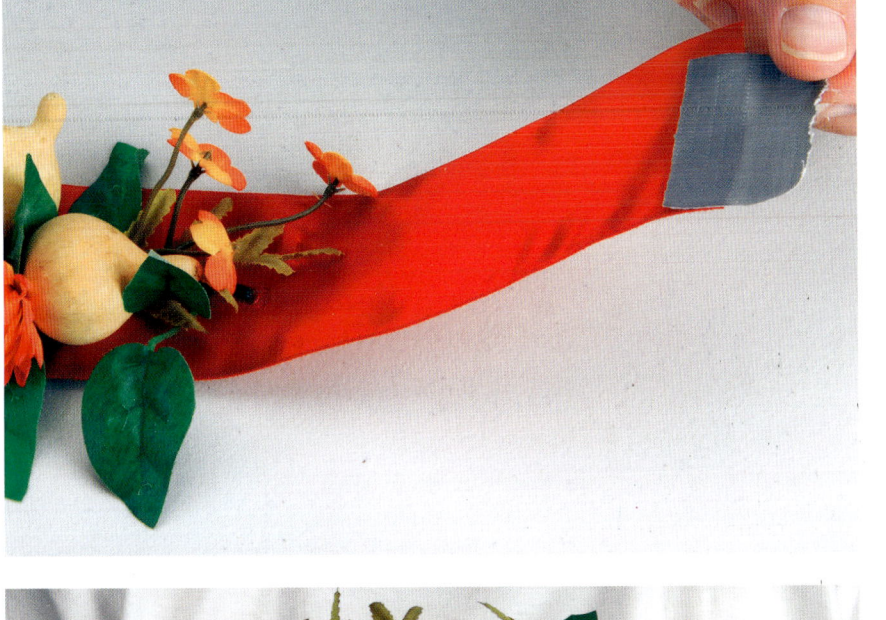

Center the decorated ribbon on the headband and check it for balance.

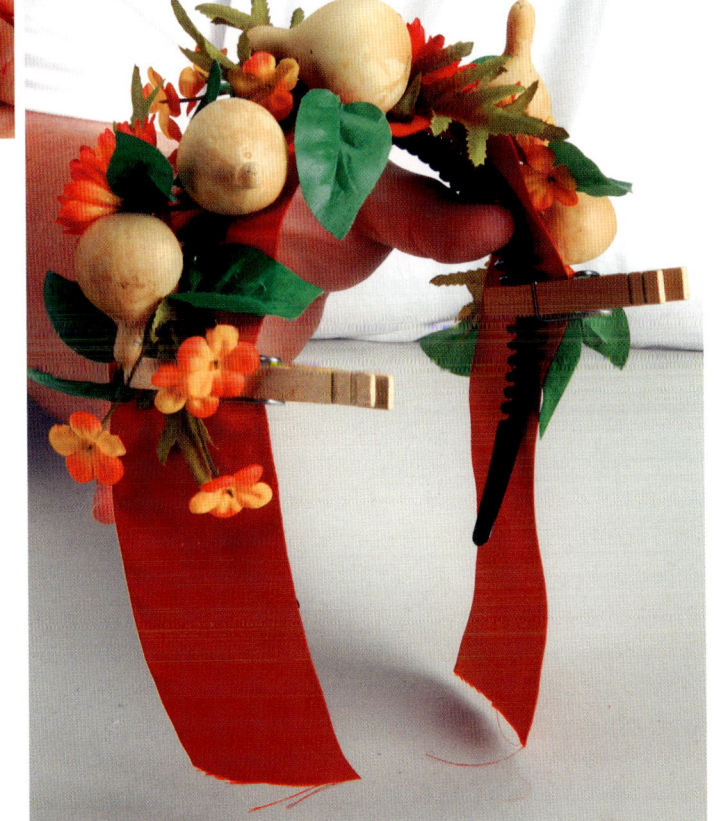

Once the ribbon is centered, use clothespins to temporarily hold the ribbon on the headband.

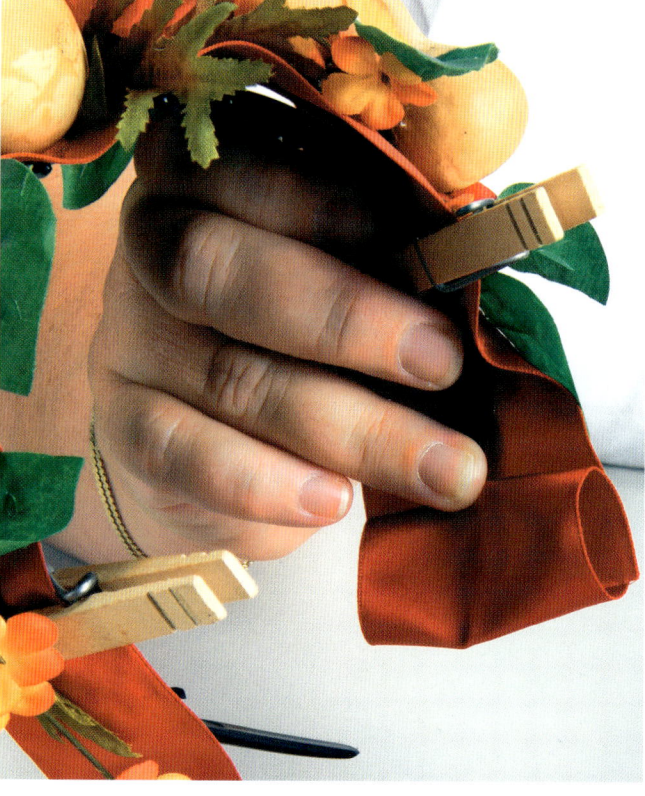

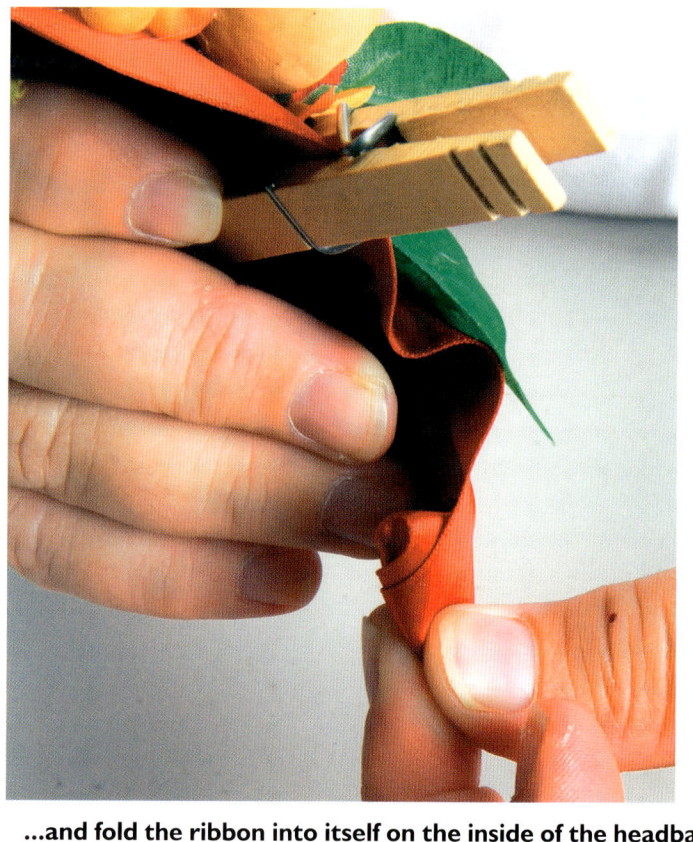

At the ends, fold the end of the ribbon around the end of the headband tip...

...and fold the ribbon into itself on the inside of the headband so the tips are covered in cloth.

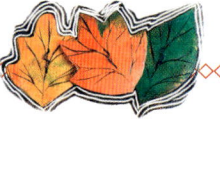

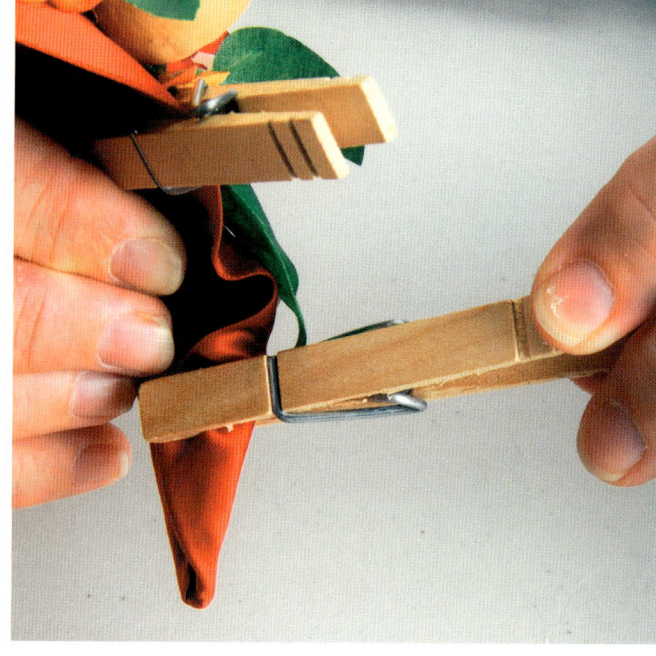

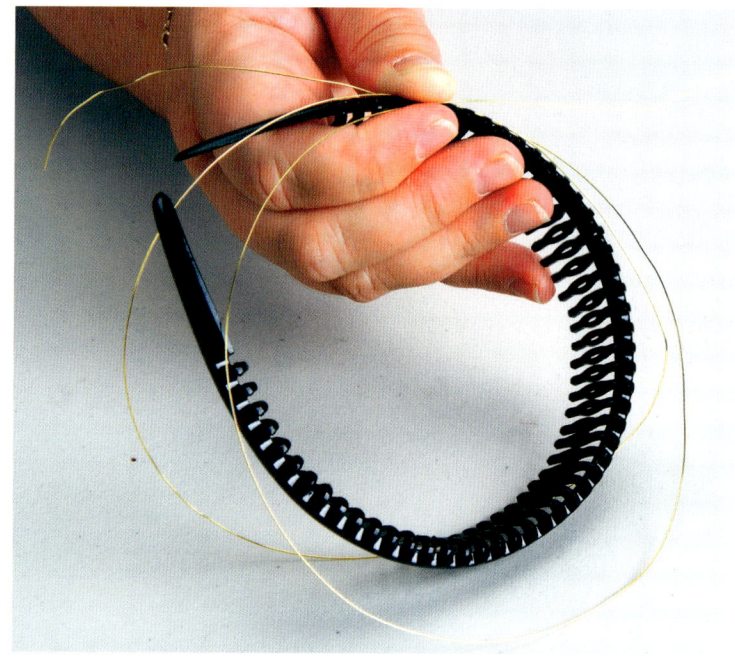

Use a clothespin to hold the ribbon in place

Cut a piece of 26-gauge brass wire that is 2½ times the length of the headband.

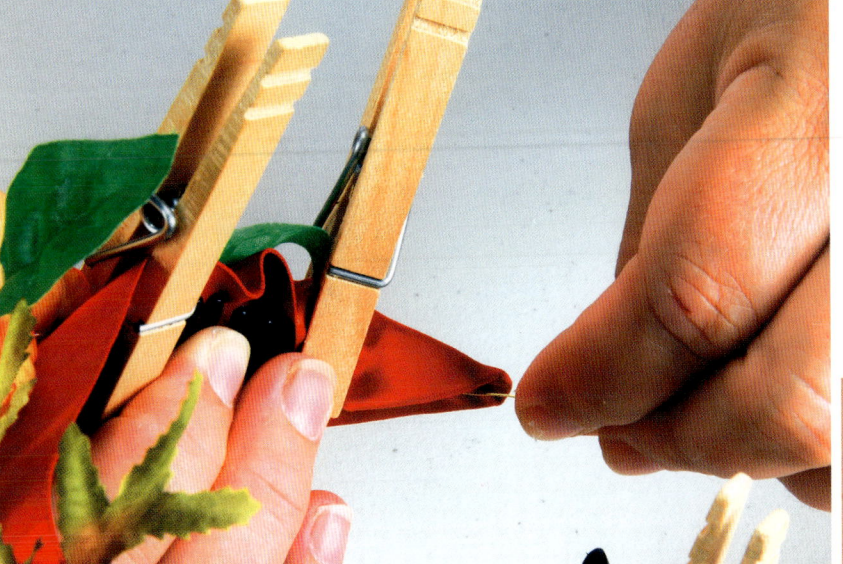

To start attaching the ribbon to the head-band, tuck 1" of the wire into the fold at one end of the headband.

Wind the wire around the headband and over its tucked-in part about four times.

Then, working in a loose winding fashion, work your way up and around the headband toward the autumn gourds and flowers/leaves, gathering and tucking the edges of the ribbon under the headband along the way.

When moving through the gourds and foliage, be sure to capture the vine stem as you wind the wire around and around.

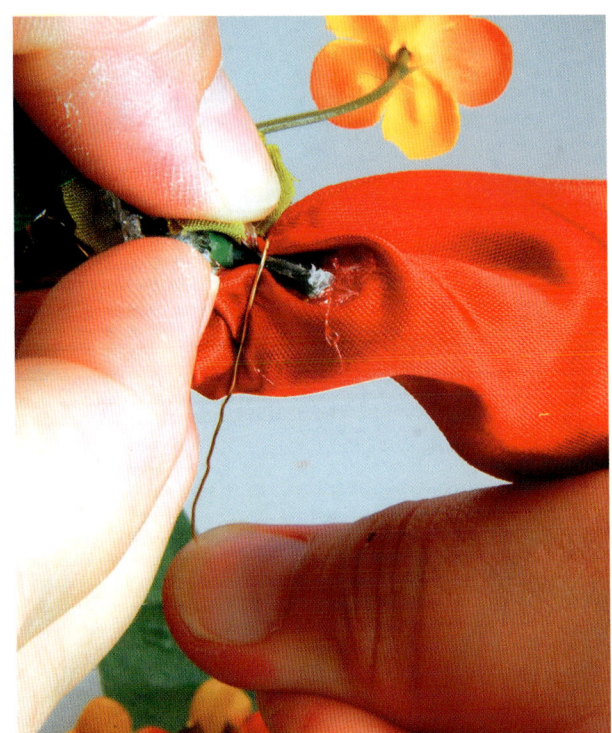

27

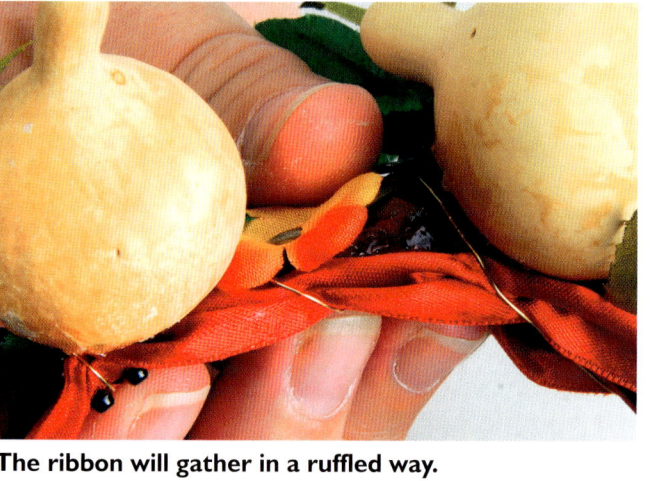

The ribbon will gather in a ruffled way.

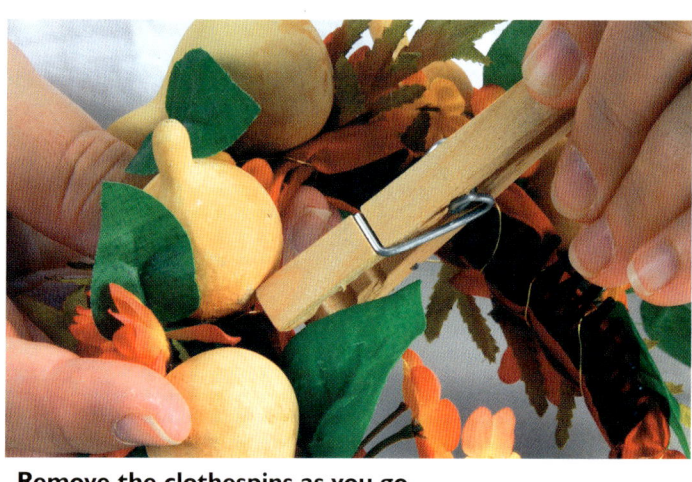

Remove the clothespins as you go.

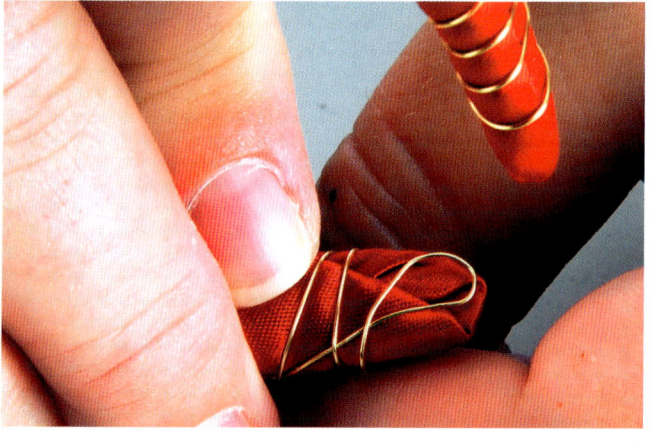

When approaching the opposite end, wind the wire ½" past the end of the folded ribbon and backwrap four times.

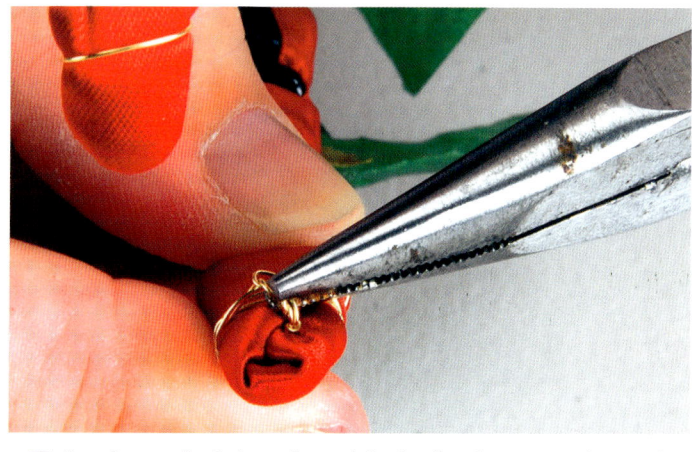

Twist the end of the wire with the backwrap, trim and tuck into the fold. Needle-nosed pliers help with this part.

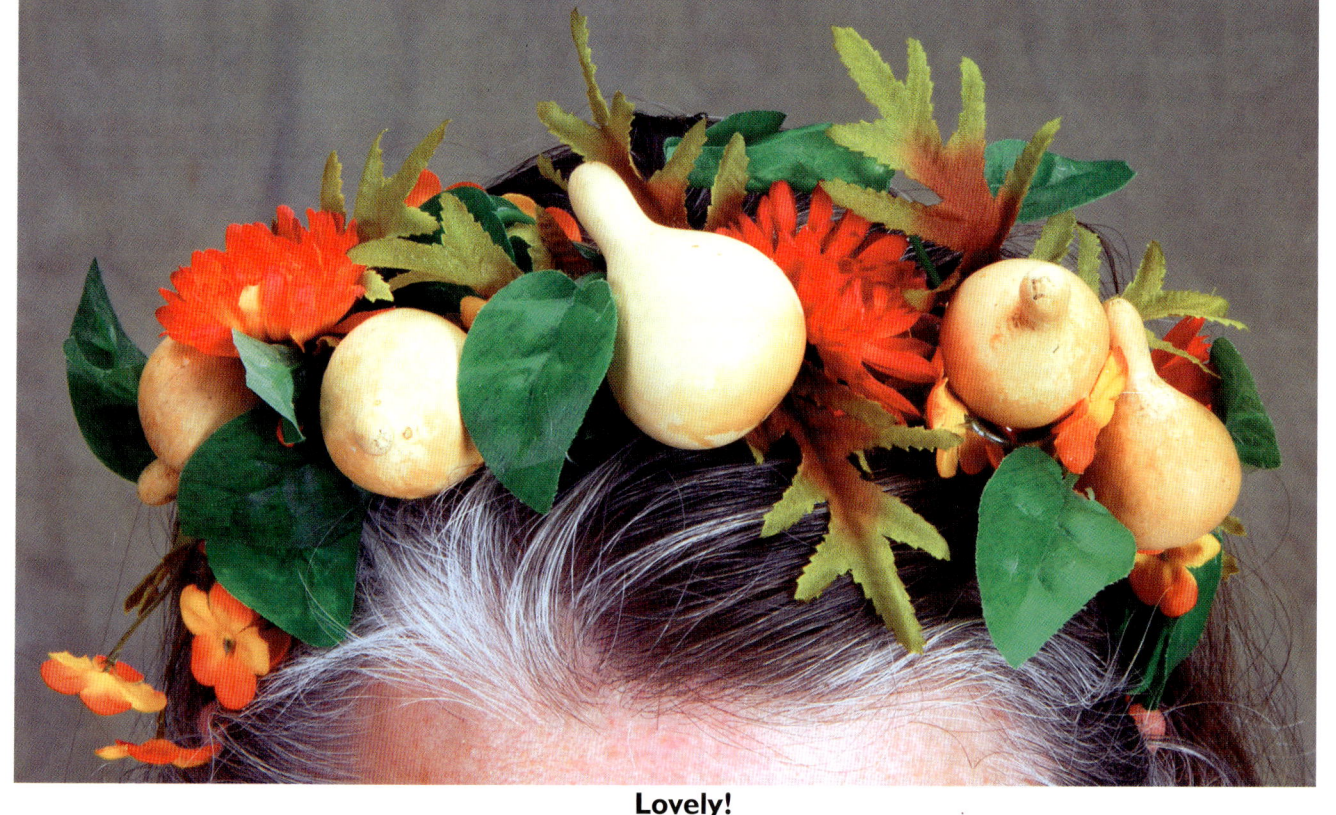

Lovely!

Hatband

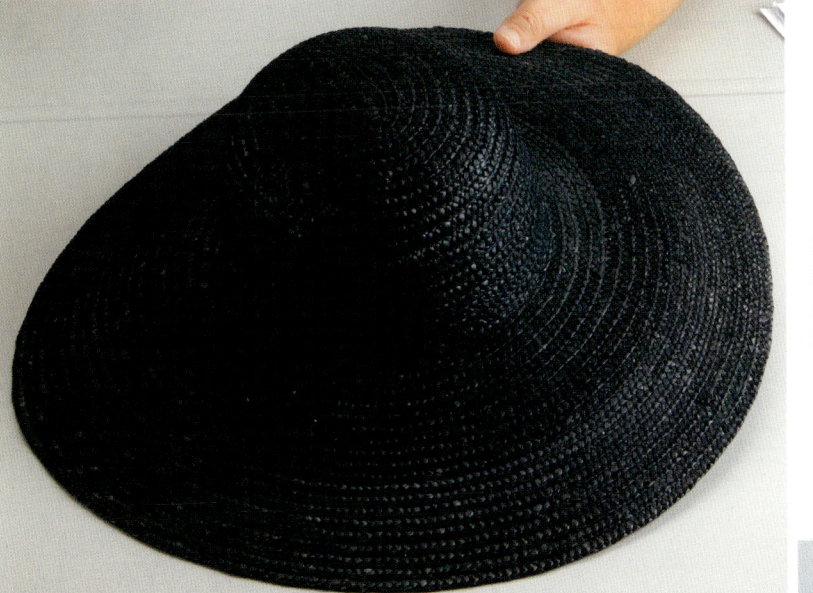

Hatbands are similar to headbands, except they are completed loops that fit around the crown of the hat. Choose a hat you would like to wear.

Gather a couple small gourds and silk flowers and/or leaves for decoration. Select some ribbon, straw braid, or raffia for the band.

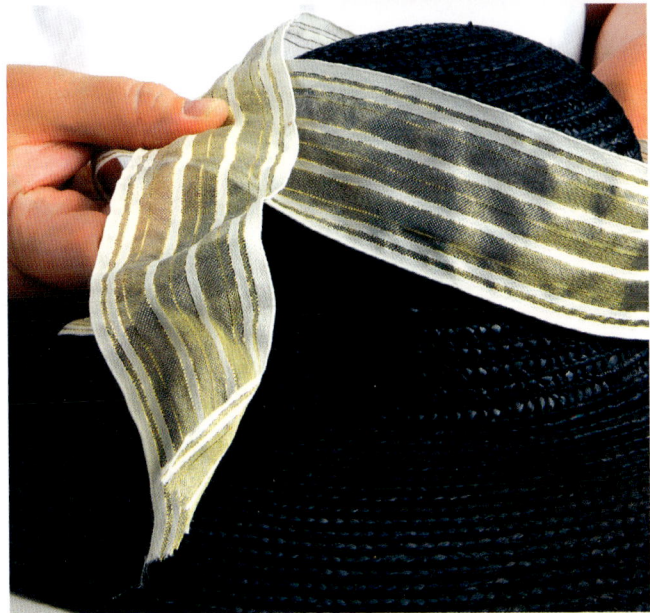

Wrap your piece of banding material around the crown of the hat, and cross at the back.

Hold the band at the crosspoint and carefully take it off.

29

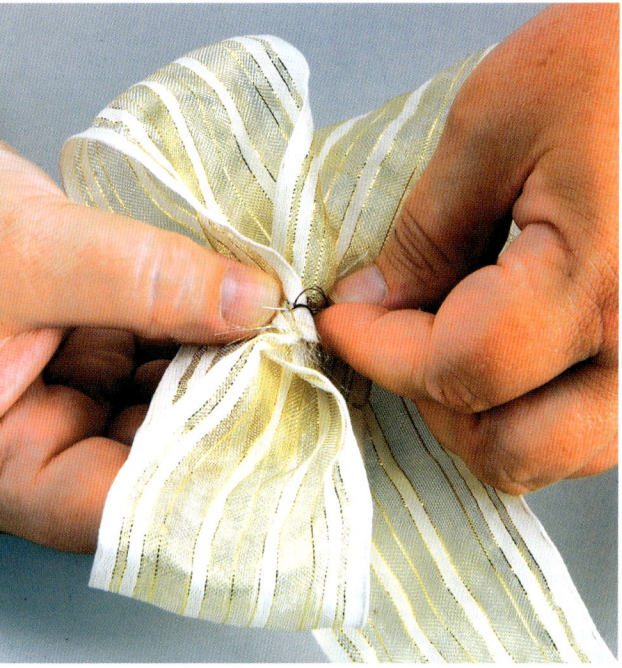

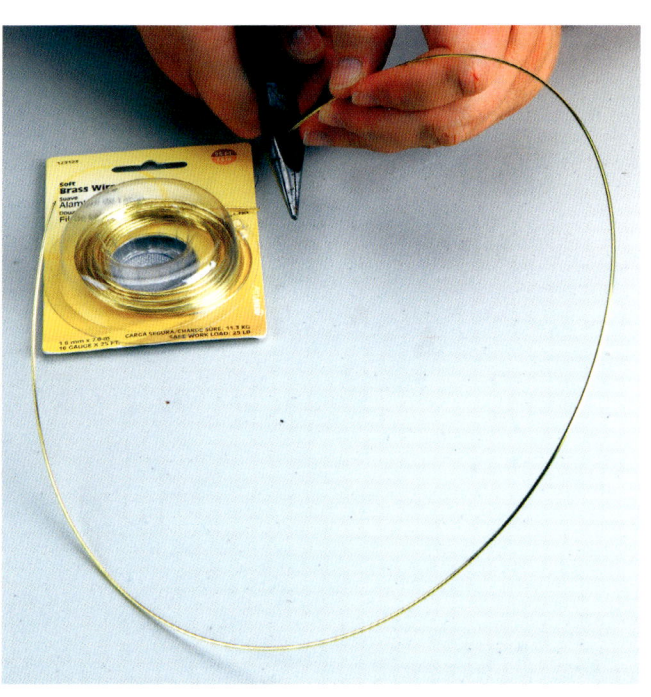

Fold the ribbon's ends to the crosspoint and make several stitches through all the layers, to secure them. Knot the thread and cut.

Cut a two-foot section of 16-gauge brass wire.

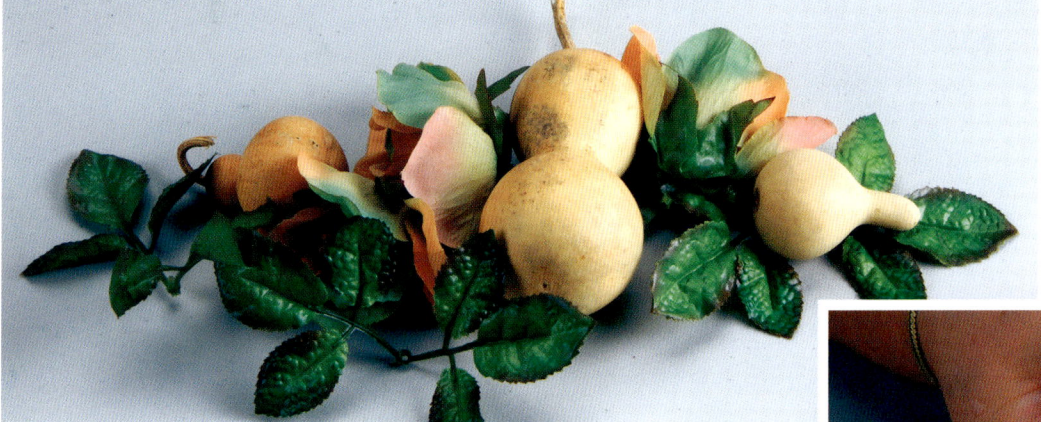

Arrange the decorations you have gathered. Keep the biggest focus—the gourd—slightly off-centered, but balanced with the other pieces.

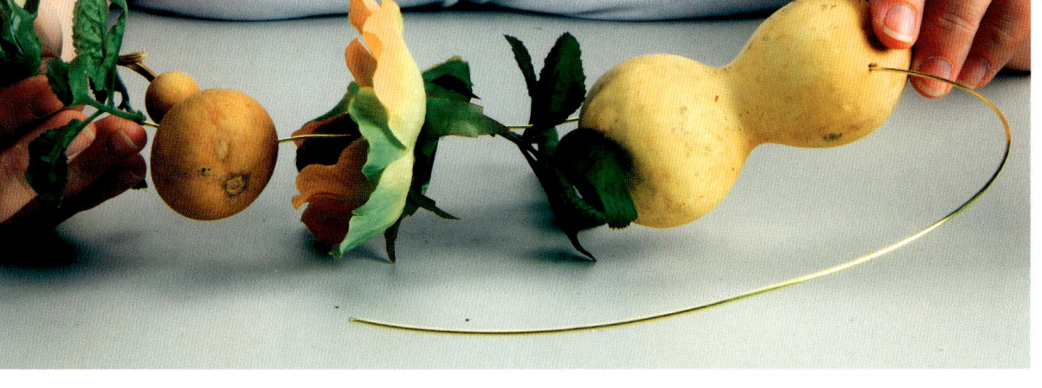

All the decorations for this particular hat will be put at the cross point, so the ribbon will be peeking out from behind the decorations. Start with the center gourd by twisting the wire through it.

Thread the leaves, flowers, and gourds on the wire on one side of the main gourd.

30

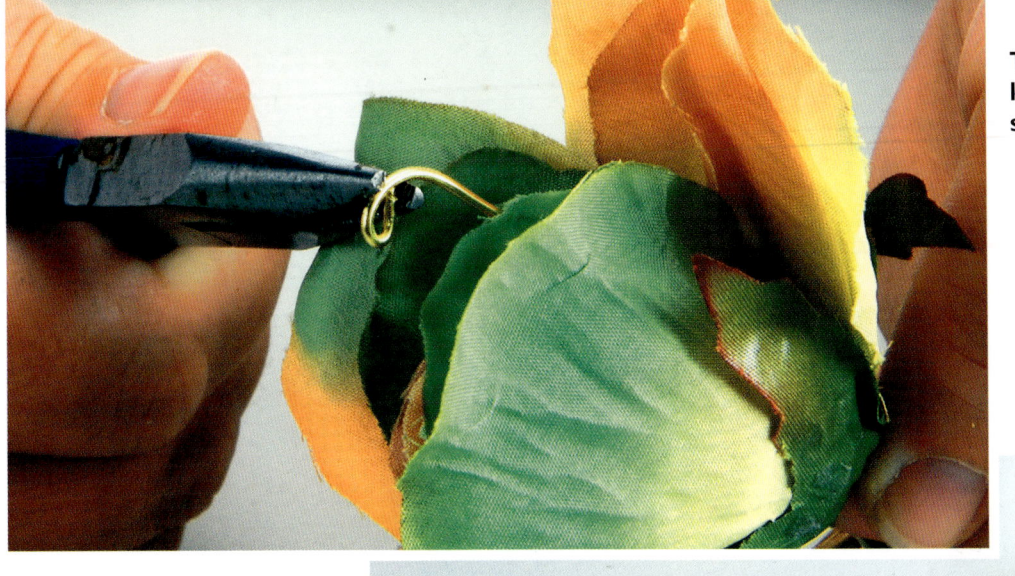

Twist the wire at its end to keep your decorations from slipping off.

Thread the other side of the main gourd with the rest of the decorative material. Take any leftover wire, and wrap it around a pencil or pen to create a 'tendril.'

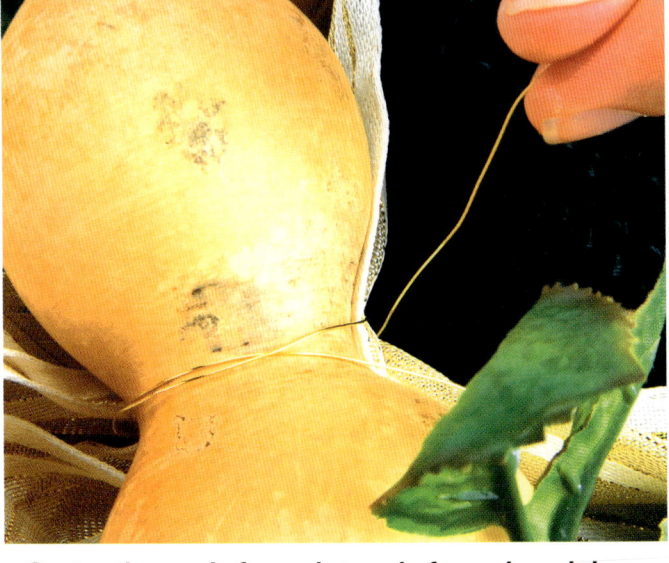

Center the newly-formed strand of gourds and decorations over the ribbon's crosspoint on the crown of the hat. Attach the strand to the ribbon with jewelry-wire.

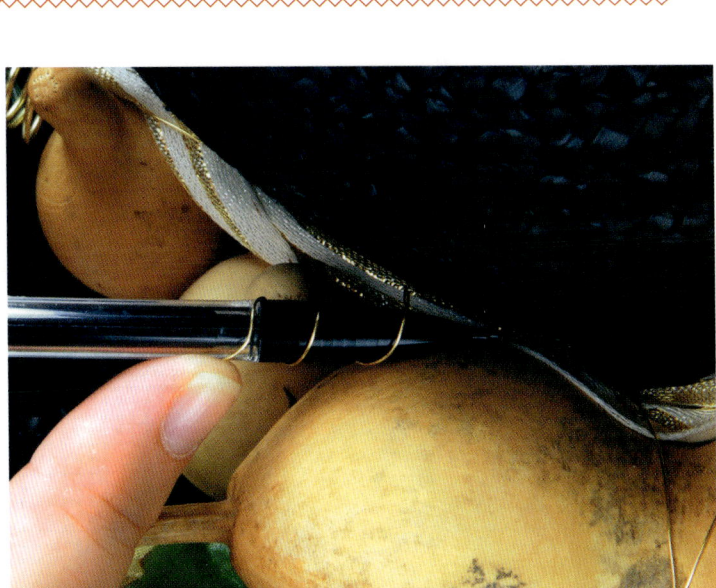

Spiral the ends of the wire around a pencil or pen to make additional 'tendrils.'

31

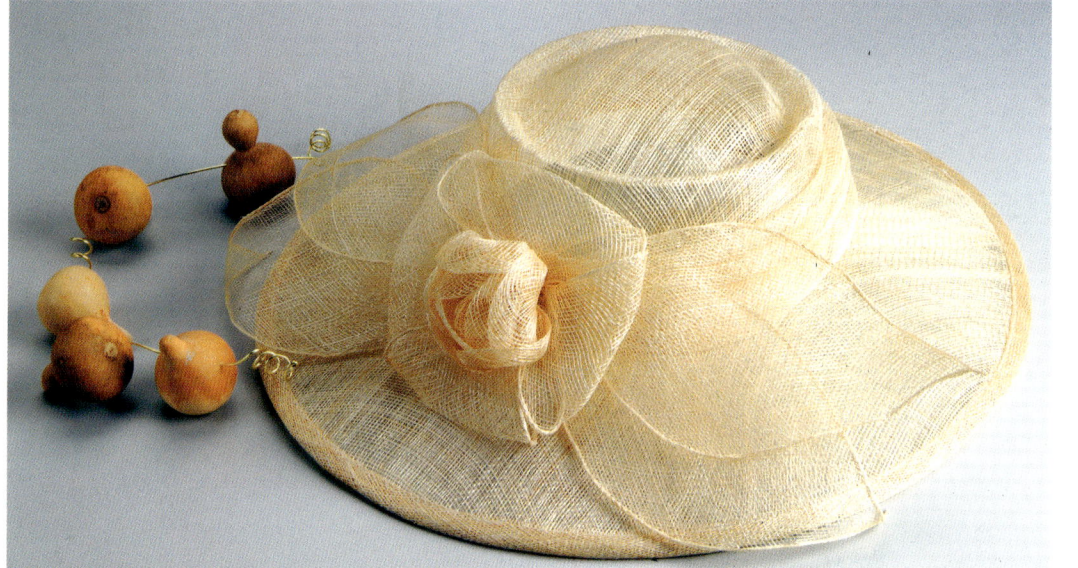

For another type of hat, use a pre-designed hat from your local shop. String an odd number of gourds onto a piece of wire.

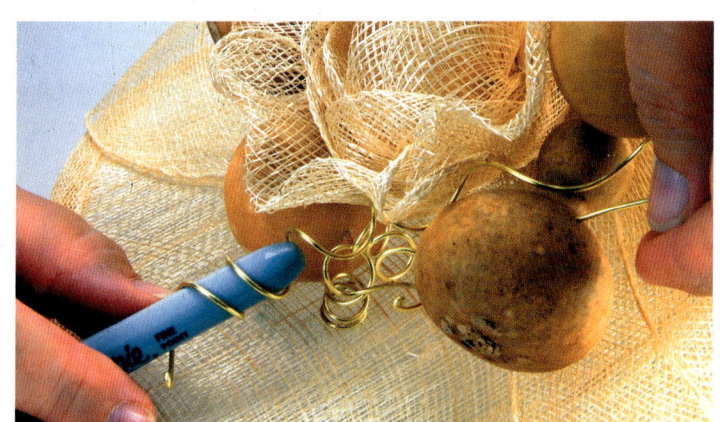

For this hat, I made a ring of gourds and brought the existing flower through it. An extra wire spiral at the bottom adds the finishing touch.

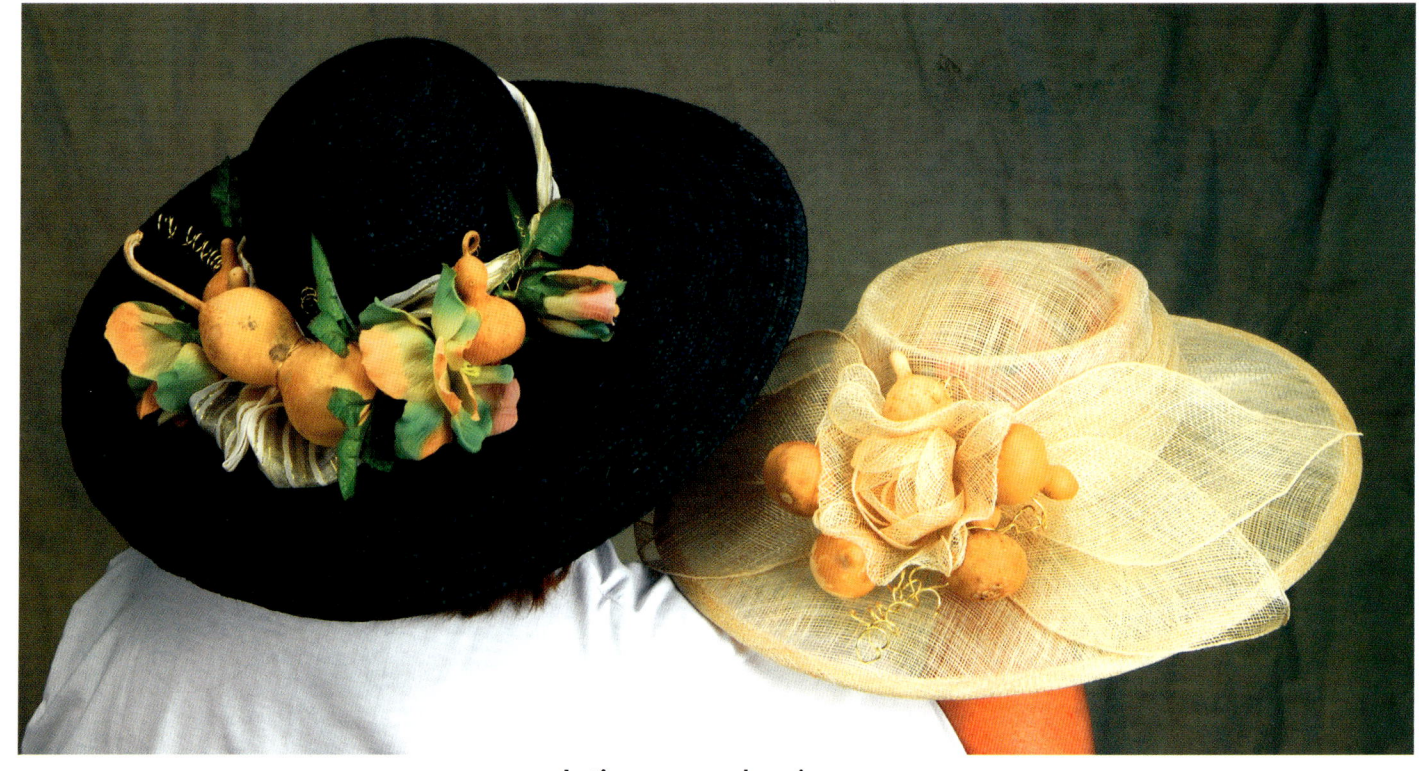

Let's go somewhere!

Caplet ◇◇

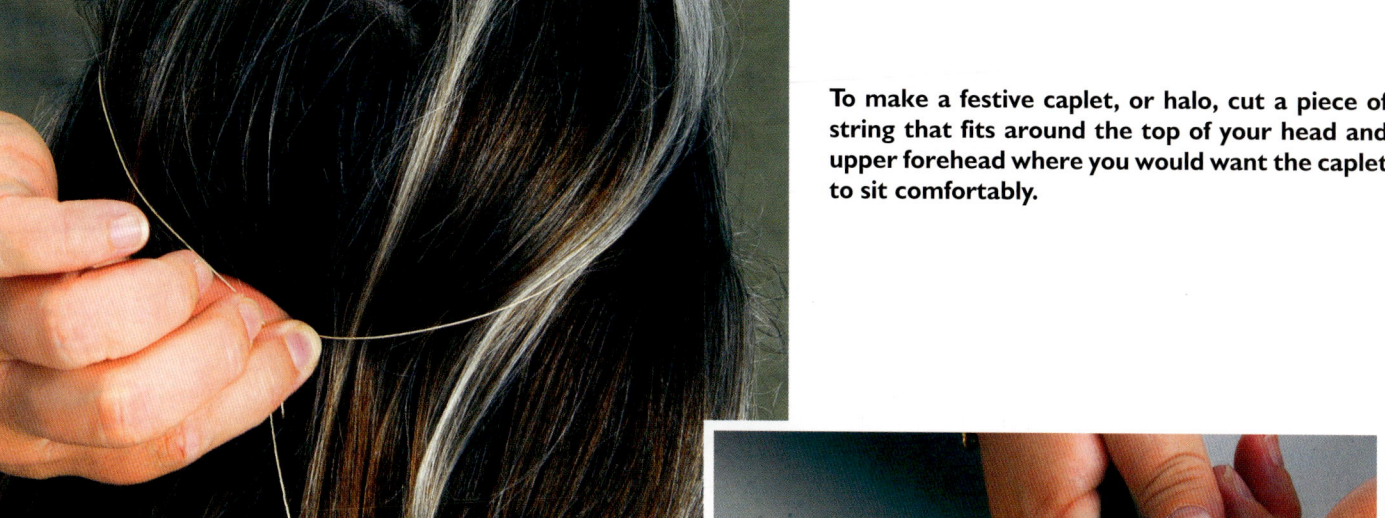

To make a festive caplet, or halo, cut a piece of string that fits around the top of your head and upper forehead where you would want the caplet to sit comfortably.

Once you have a measurement that works, cut a piece of wire a little more than twice that length. I'm using a piece of 16-gauge brass wire.

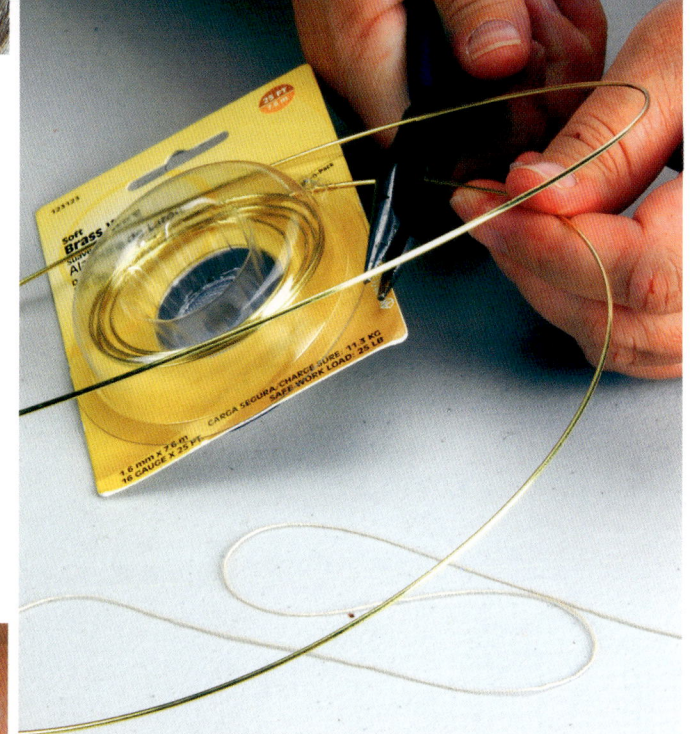

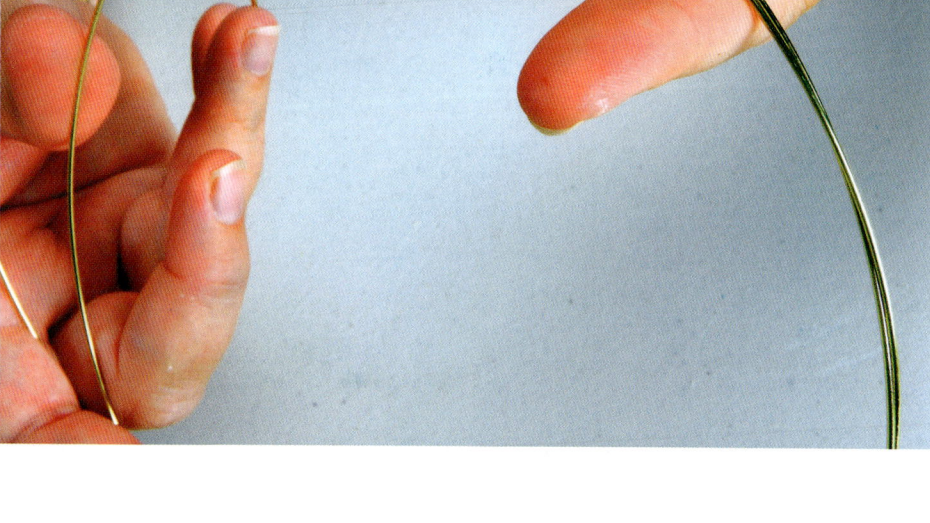

Turn the wire into a double circle, and loosely twist the wire together.

33

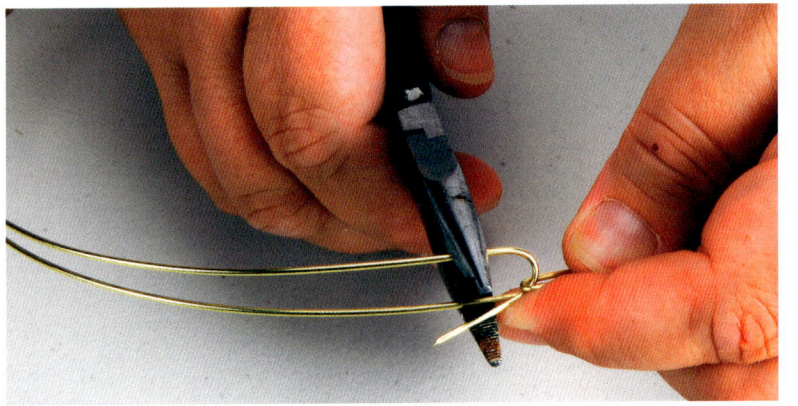

Hook the ends through the loop at the opposite end and pinch shut to make a hoop. The hooked ends are the front centerpoint of the hoop.

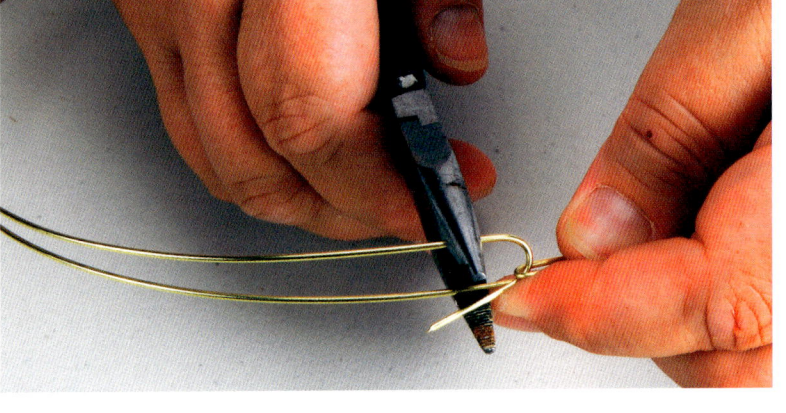

Line up a selection of artificial foliage and mini-gourds that are roughly the same length as the piece of string used to measure your head. Trim all the stems to a 3" length.

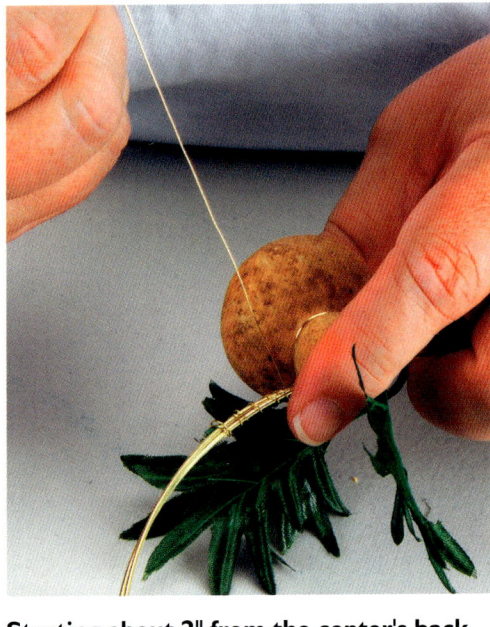

Starting about 2" from the center's back, use a spool of gold-colored jewelry wire to spiral-wrap the mini-gourds, flowers, and leaves to the hoop. There will be an open area on the center back of the hoop.

As you pass the halfway mark on the first stem, add the next stem from your lineup of decorations. Keep wrapping.

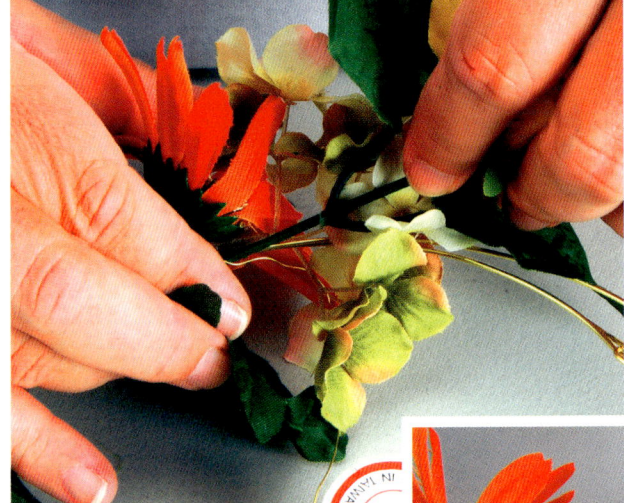

Notice how I spiraled the wire around this gourd instead of going through it.

34

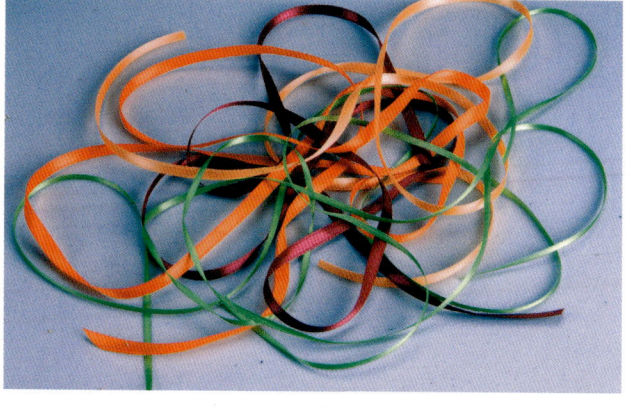

When all the items have been attached, cut an odd number of ¼" to 1" ribbons, each about 3-5' long.

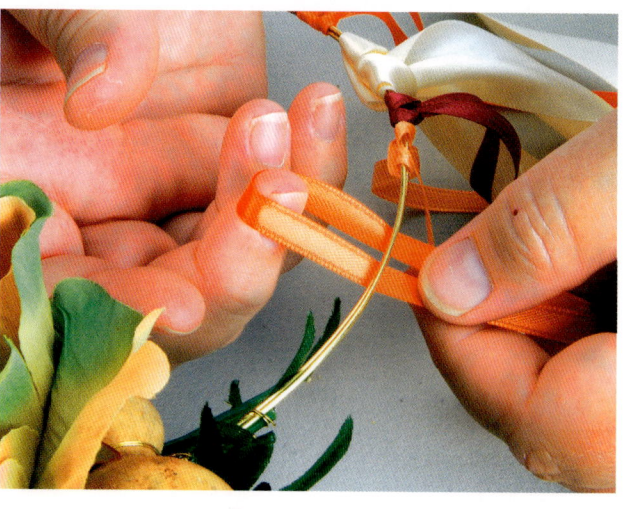

In the open area at the back of the caplet, fold the ribbon under the hoop...

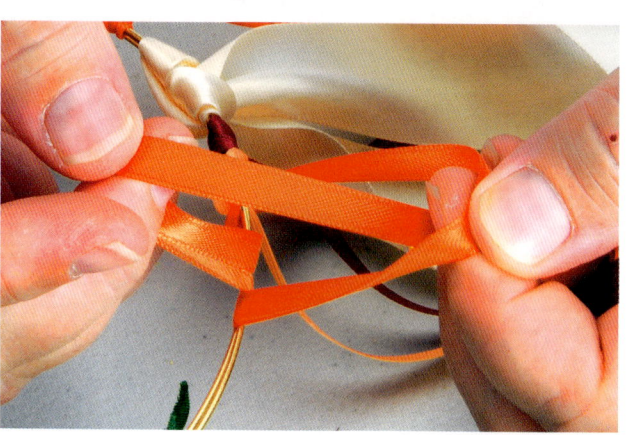

...and bring the ends through the fold.

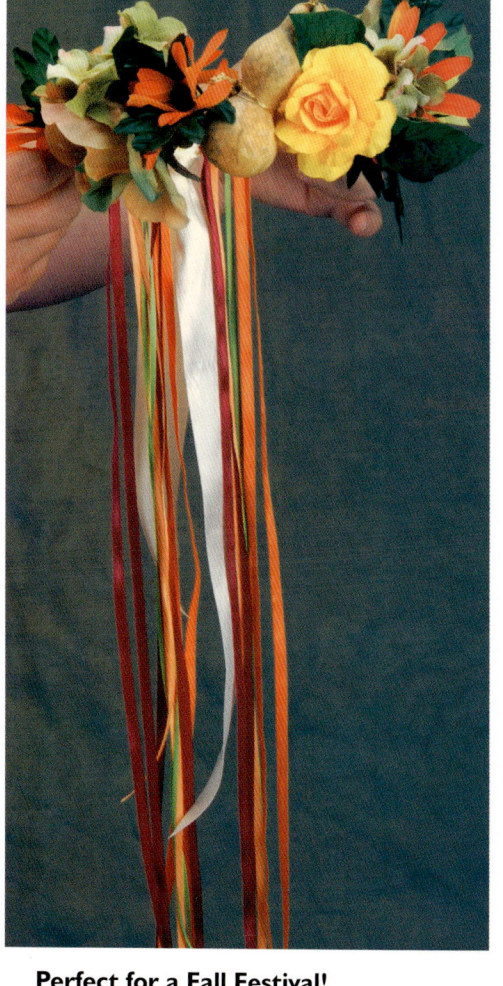

Continue adding ribbons, to suit your taste. Hold the hoop upright and dot each ribbon knot with glue.

Perfect for a Fall Festival!

35

Hatpins ◇◇◇

Hatpins are time-honored tools for keeping a hat from blowing away on a windy day and are routinely used for other purposes such as lapel pins and scarf clasps. Using beads and gourds can make a simple tool something worthy of display as a lovely addition to an autumn outfit.

Let's be a fashion statement!

Hatpins are so easy I'm almost embarrassed to show them to you. First, select some mini-gourds with shapes you like, some matching beads, and a foot or so of the brass jewelry wire we've been using all along.

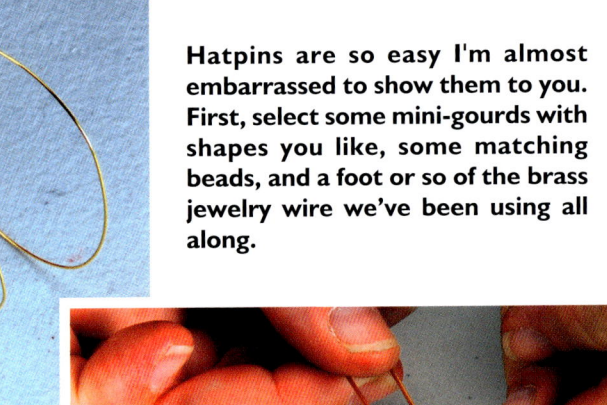

Hatpin wires can be purchased through jewelry supply centers or mail order catalogs. They have a blunt pinhead end and a pointed opposite end with a stop button.

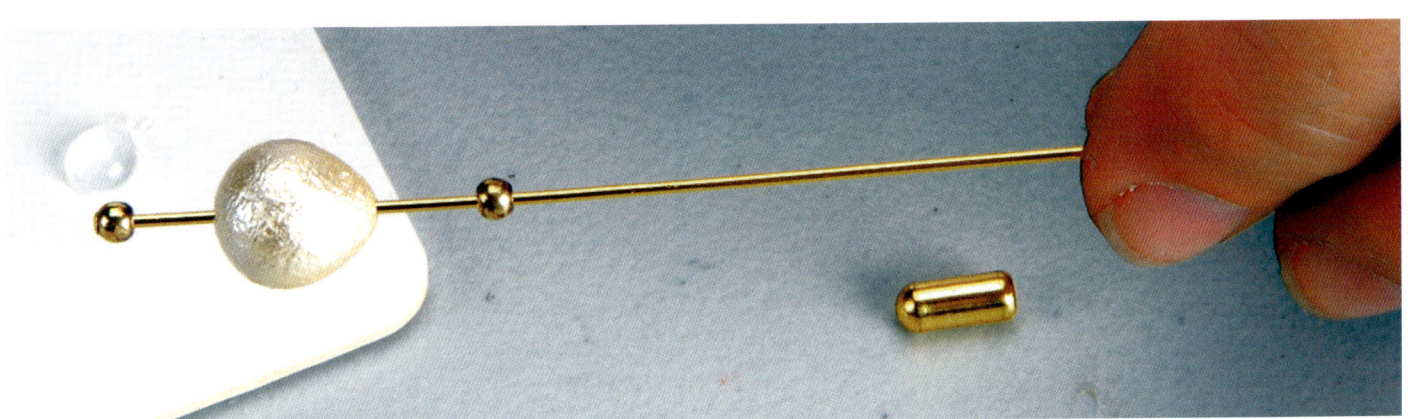

To begin, take off the stop button. Put a bead or two onto the hatpin...

36

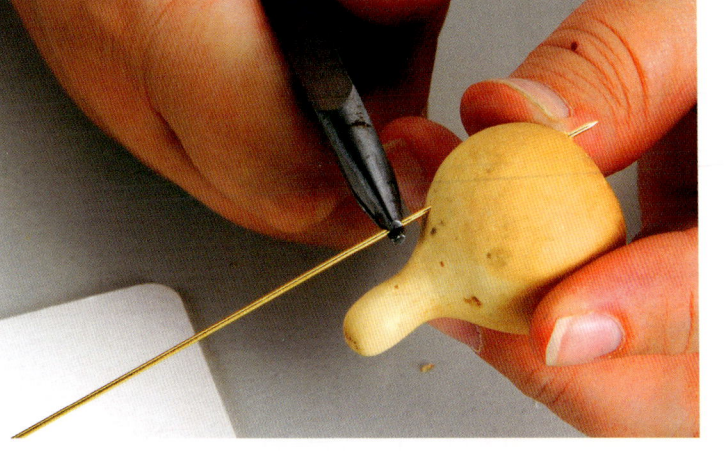

...followed by the gourd. I pierce the gourd with the hatpin using pliers toward the back third of the gourd so the bulk of it is on one side of the hatpin. That way, it will sit flatter against the hat or lapel.

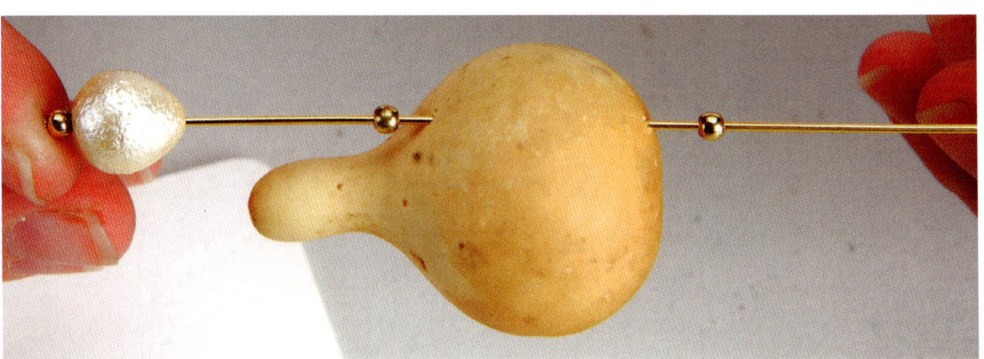

End with a bead.

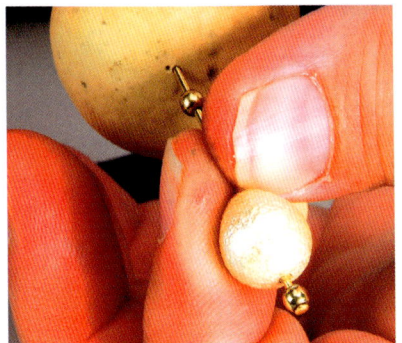

Starting with the first bead, use a toothpick and place a small dot of E6000 glue on the hatpin; slide the bead over it, toward the end.

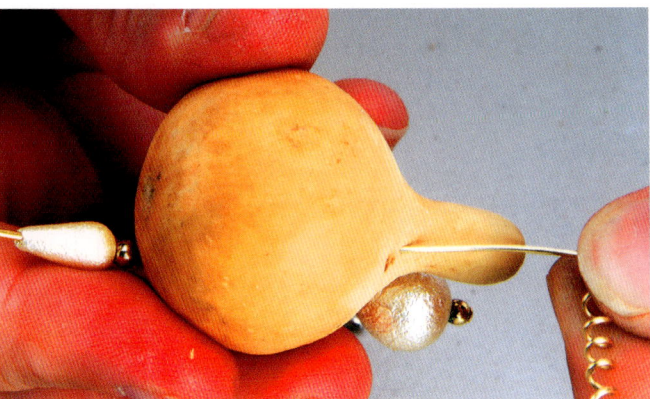

Twist the opposite end into the upper part of the gourd...

Continue with each bead and the gourd, until finished. Then let dry.

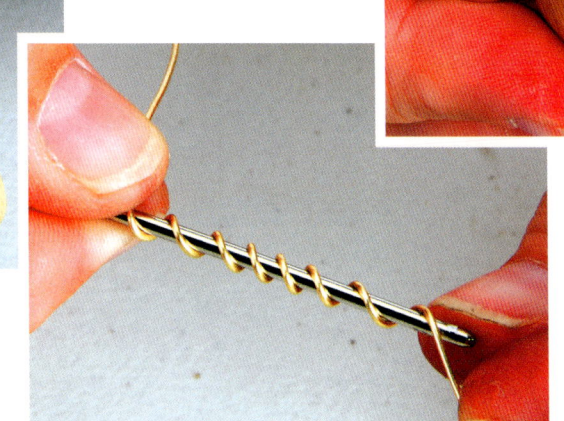

After the glue has dried, cut a 6" piece of brass jewelry wire and curl half of it around a darning needle.

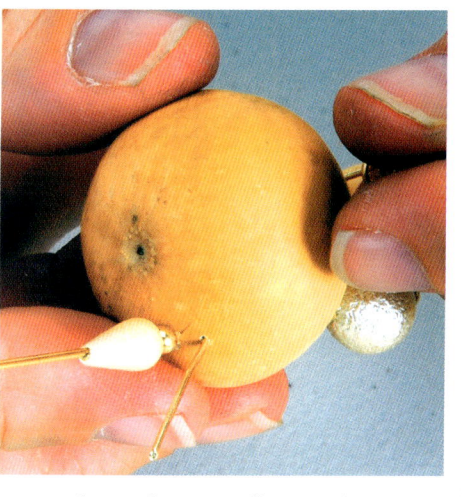 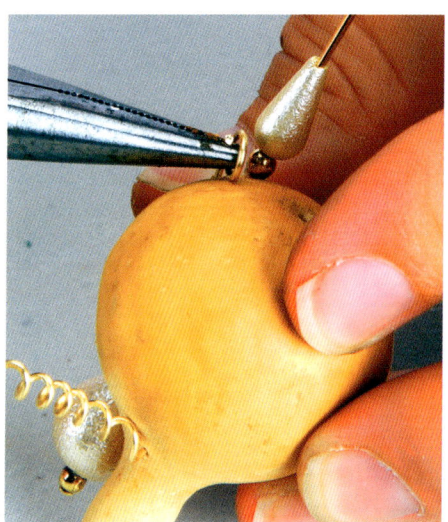 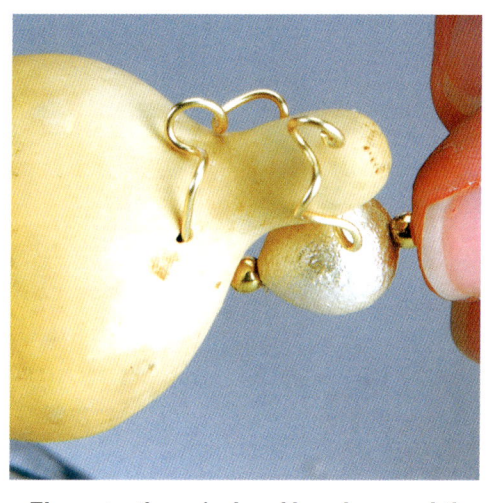

...and continue until you pierce the lower part of the gourd, somewhere near the bottom beads.

Curl the tip of the wire at the bottom of the gourd.

Elongate the spiral and bend around the gourd to resemble a vine ringlet.

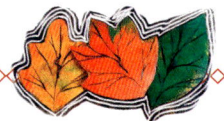

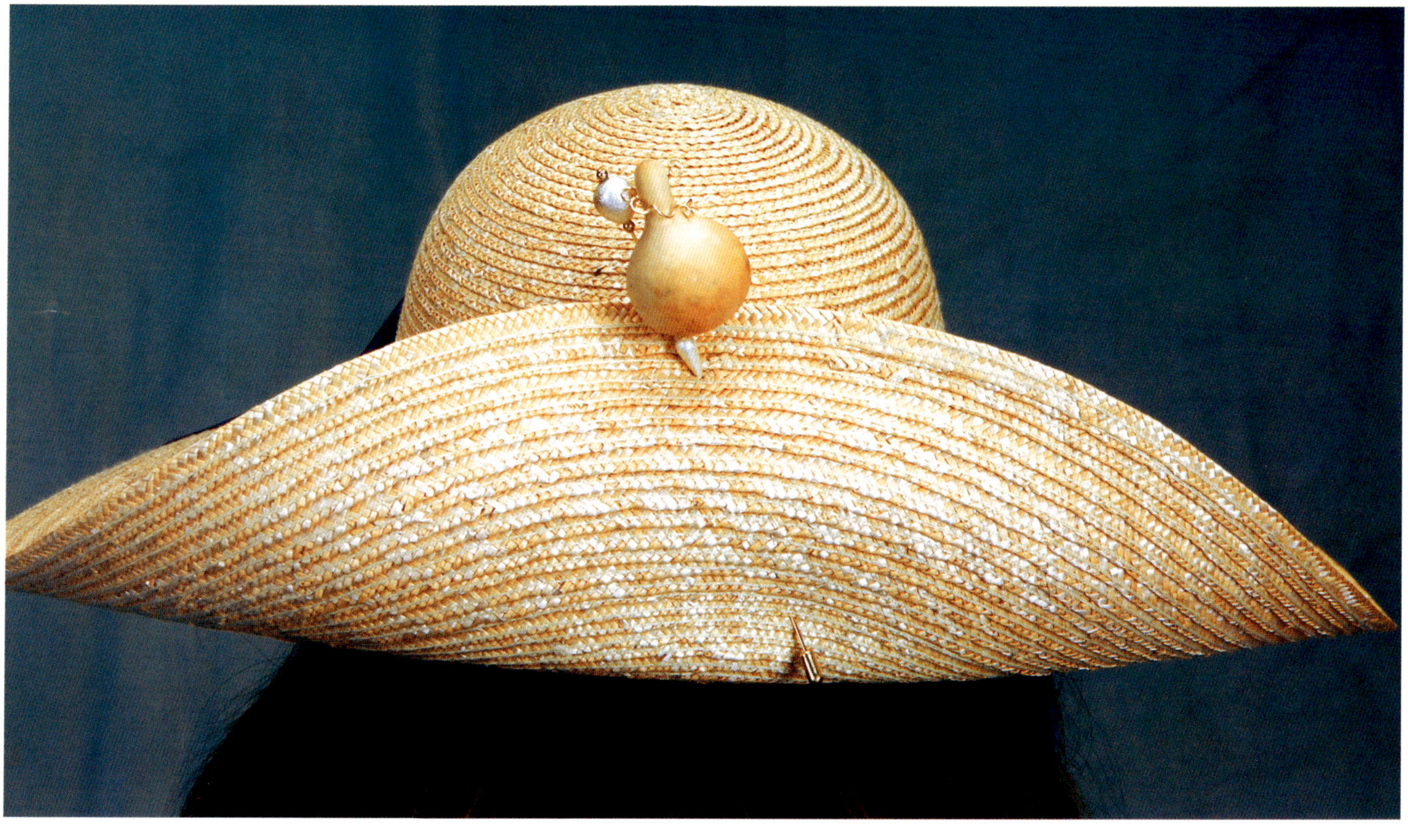

I like it!

Chapter Four:

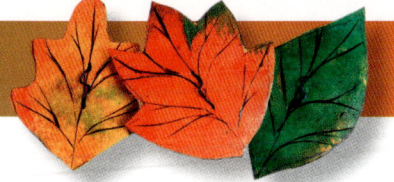

Barrettes

Gourd hair barrettes can be easily made using scraps of gourd and the proper jewelry hardware bought in craft stores. Barrettes can be wired, sown, or hot-glued to the gourd scrap. I am not a particular fan of hot-glue because if a person wears the barrette and spends the day in the sun, the glue integrity is compromised and the attached pieces will fall off. We will be wiring or tying pieces of gourd to the hardware, so that the heat from the sun will not be a problem. However, bonding glues can be fast and permanent. I use E6000 and have been pleased so far. We will also be using different art techniques for our barrettes so you can see how various media affects the look of a barrette.

Let's hold some hair!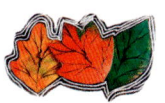

A Gourd Barrette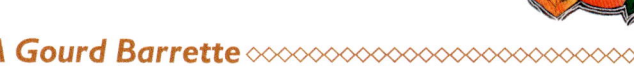

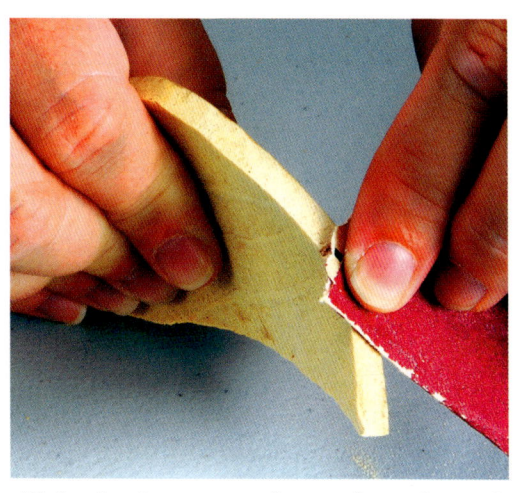

To begin a barrette, select a piece of gourd scrap with a gentle curve and sand the edges smooth.

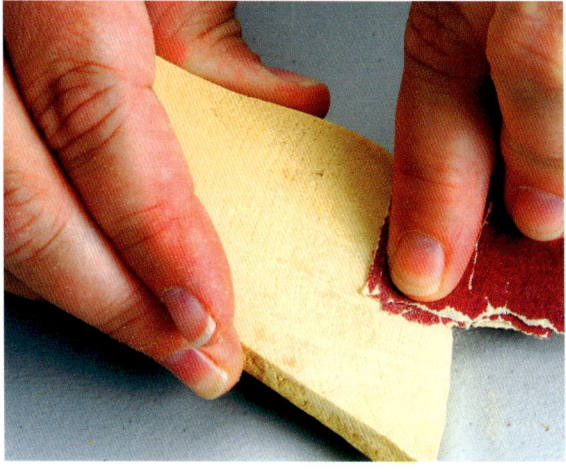

Scrape and sand the backside (interior) of the gourd until smooth.

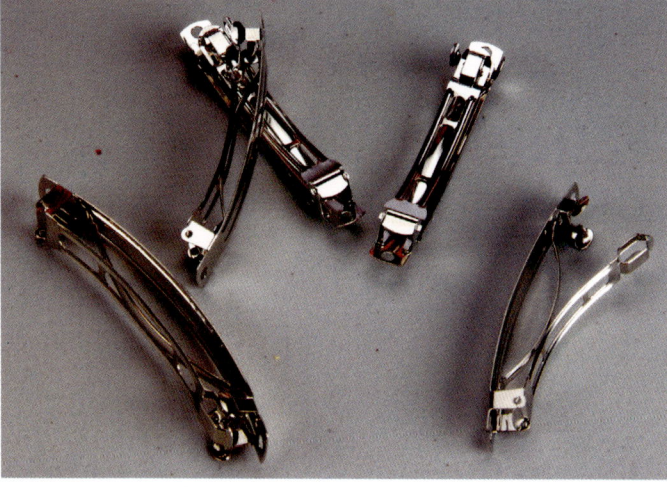

A simple gourd-made barrette is a plain gourd scrap with a regular barrette wired to it in a decorative design. Here are some examples of regular barrettes.

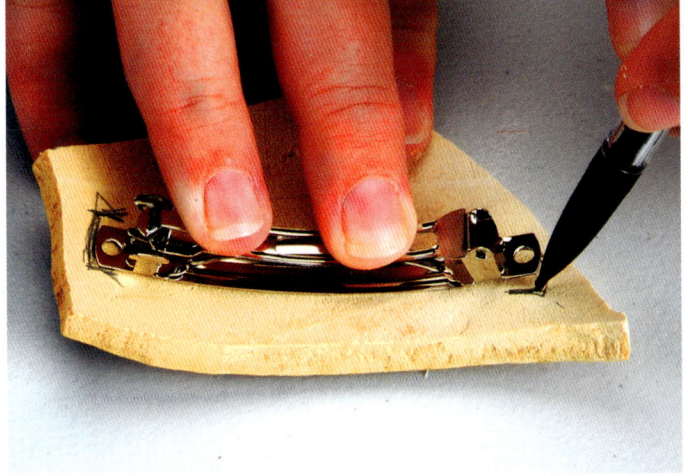

Start by tracing the placement of the barrette's ends across the underside of the scrap with a pencil. Mark the holes.

39

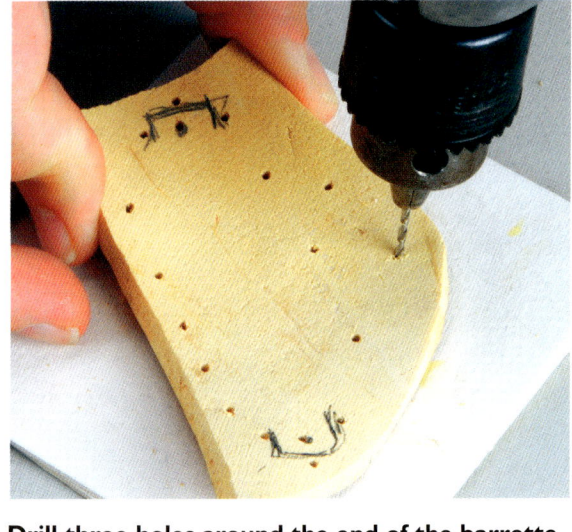

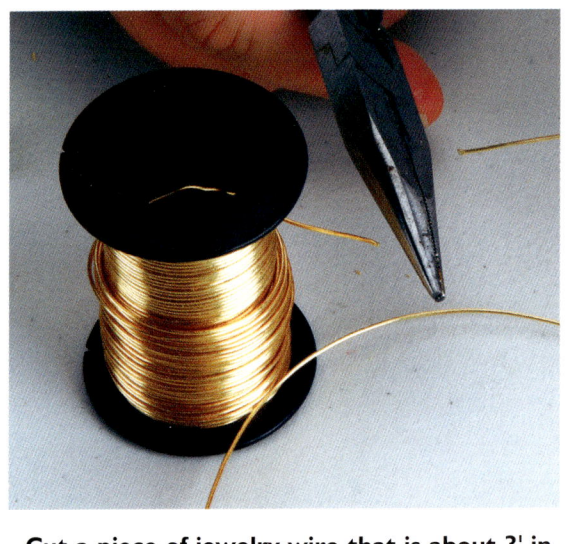

Drill three holes around the end of the barrette, through the barrette hole, and at random places on the underside of the scrap.

Cut a piece of jewelry wire that is about 3' in length. *NOTE: This particular wire is 20-gauge brass.*

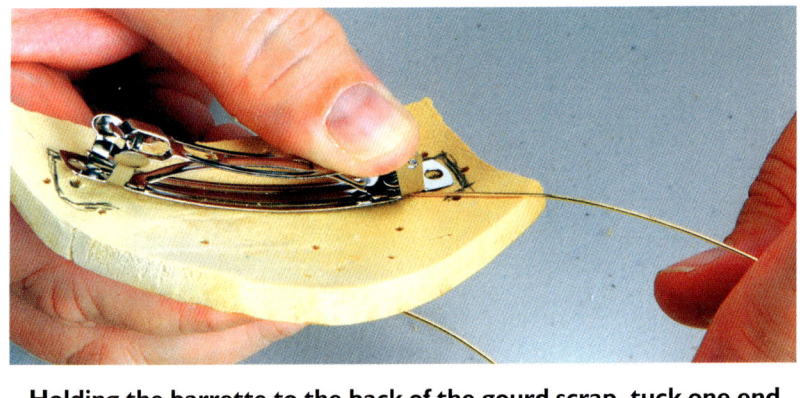

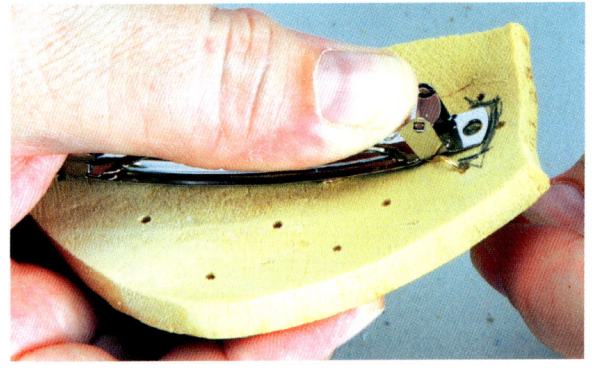

Holding the barrette to the back of the gourd scrap, tuck one end of the wire behind one end of the barrette.

Take the other end of the wire and sew through the nearest hole.

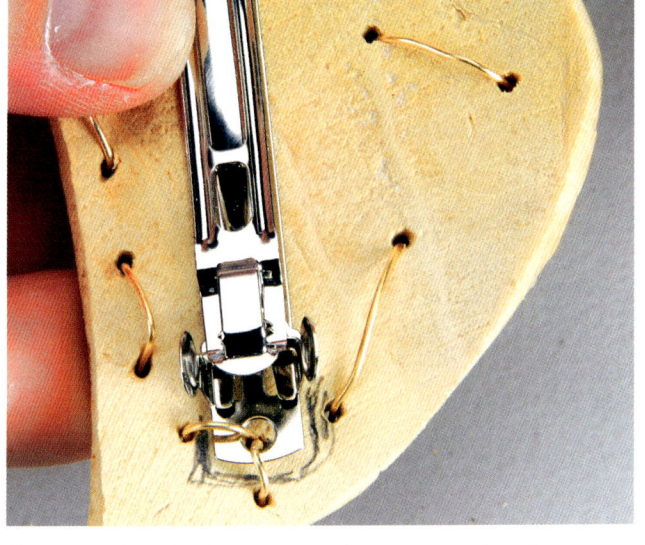

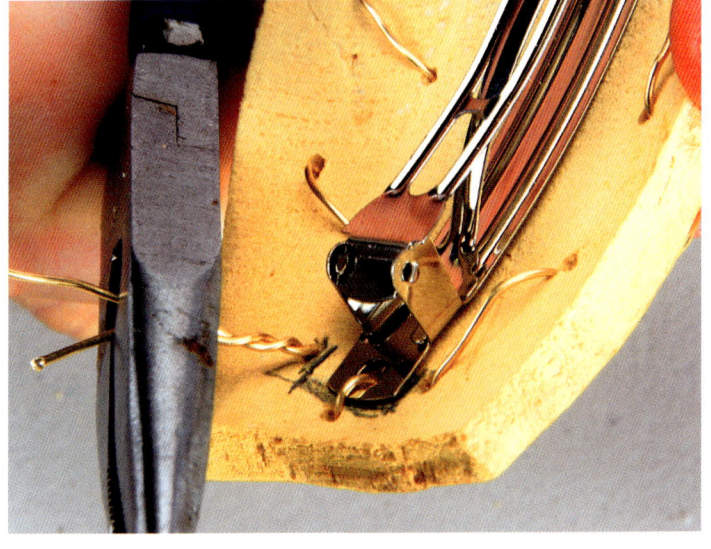

Start sewing the barrette to the scrap, going through the holes, and catching the random holes as you work around the piece.

As you get back to the beginning, untuck the original end, twist it with the new end, and trim.

40

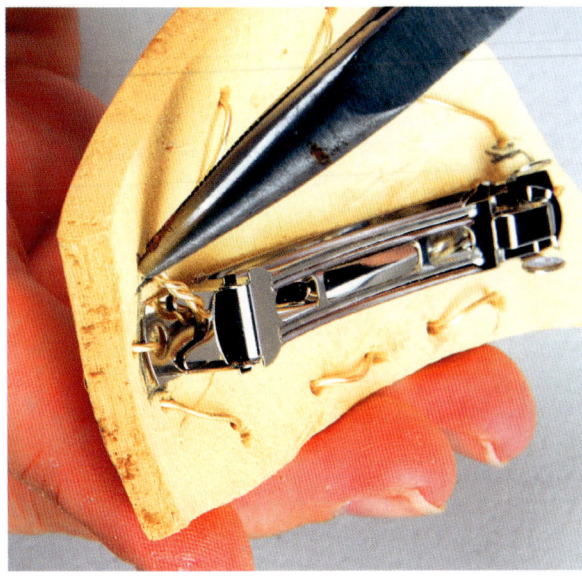 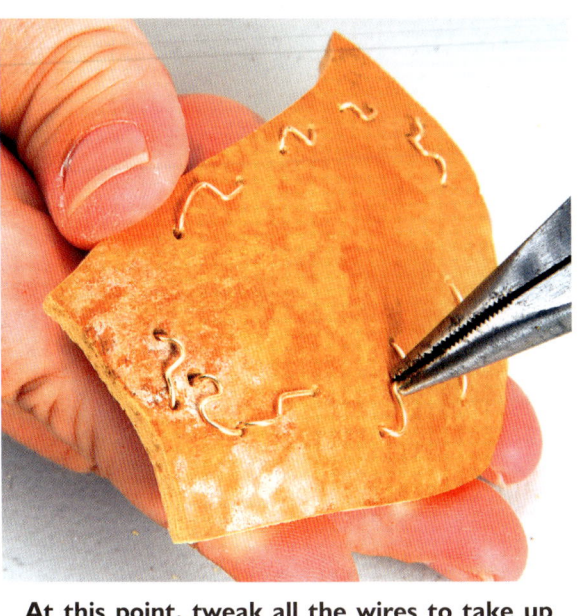

Using the tip of your pliers, bend the twist out of the way.

At this point, tweak all the wires to take up slack. This will tighten the barrette to the gourd scrap, and also put an interesting design into the sewing.

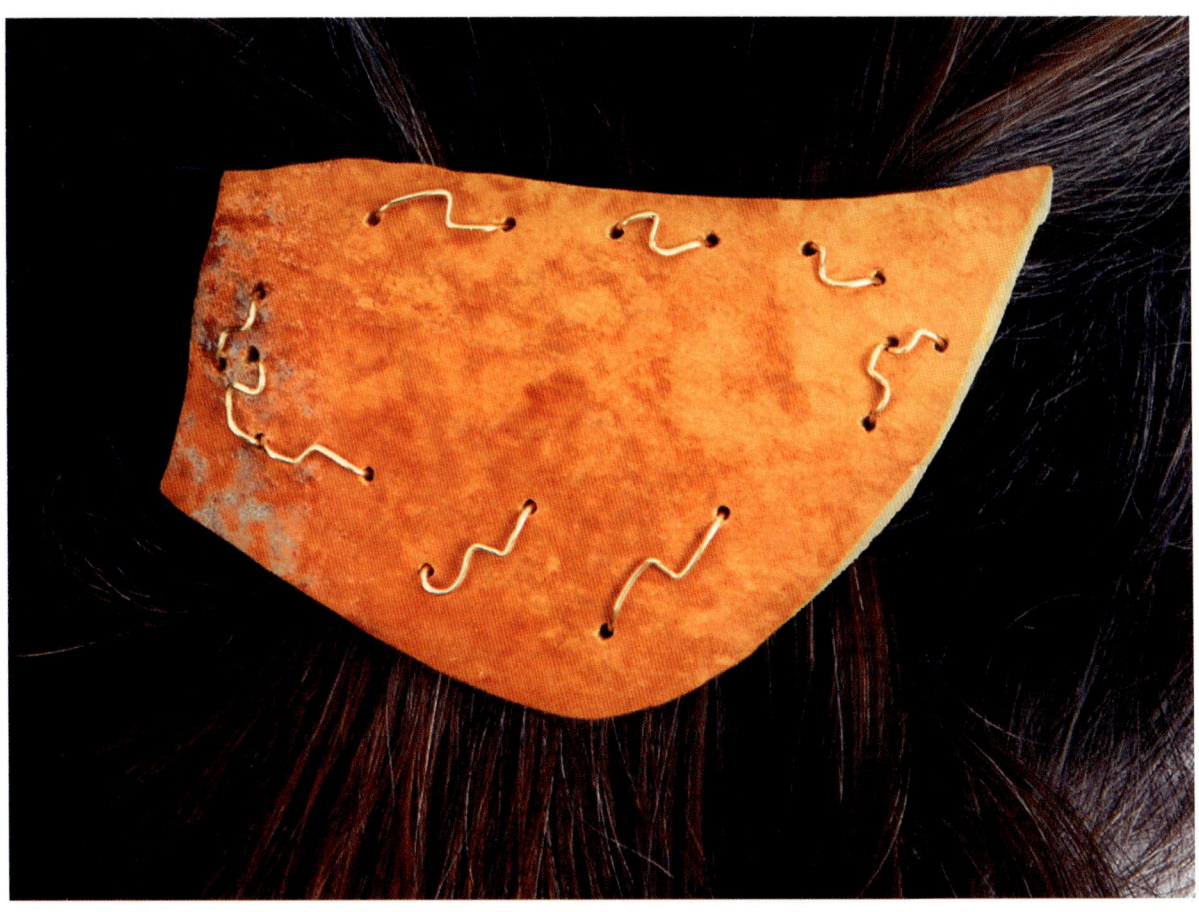

The finished barrette! Different color wires will give a different effect.

A Gourd-decorated Barrette ◇◇◇◇◇◇◇◇◇◇◇◇◇◇◇◇◇◇◇◇◇◇◇◇◇◇◇◇◇◇◇◇◇◇◇◇

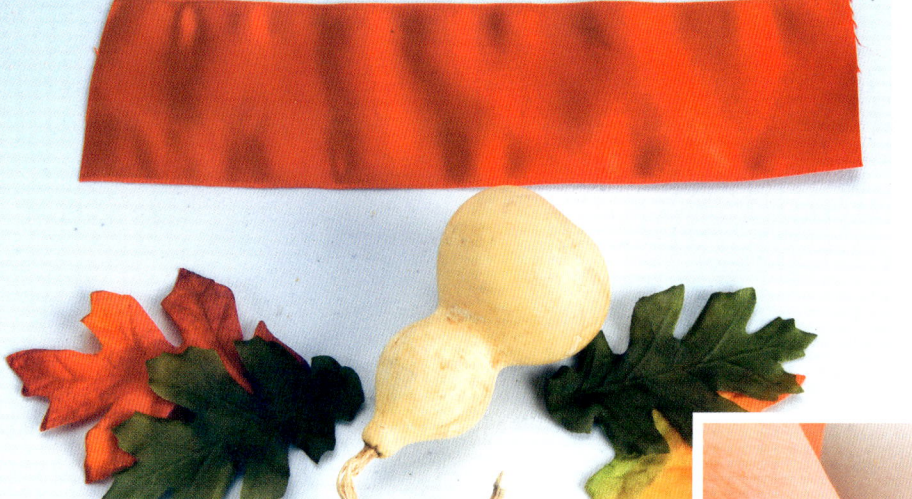

Another style involves a 2" wide piece of satin ribbon 6" long, one mini-gourd, and four small silk maple leaves. Choose a harvest-colored ribbon to match the leaves and mini-gourd.

With a needle and thread, make a running stitch across the center of the ribbon.

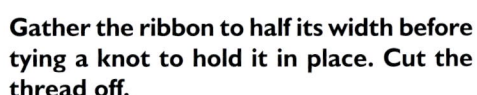

Gather the ribbon to half its width before tying a knot to hold it in place. Cut the thread off.

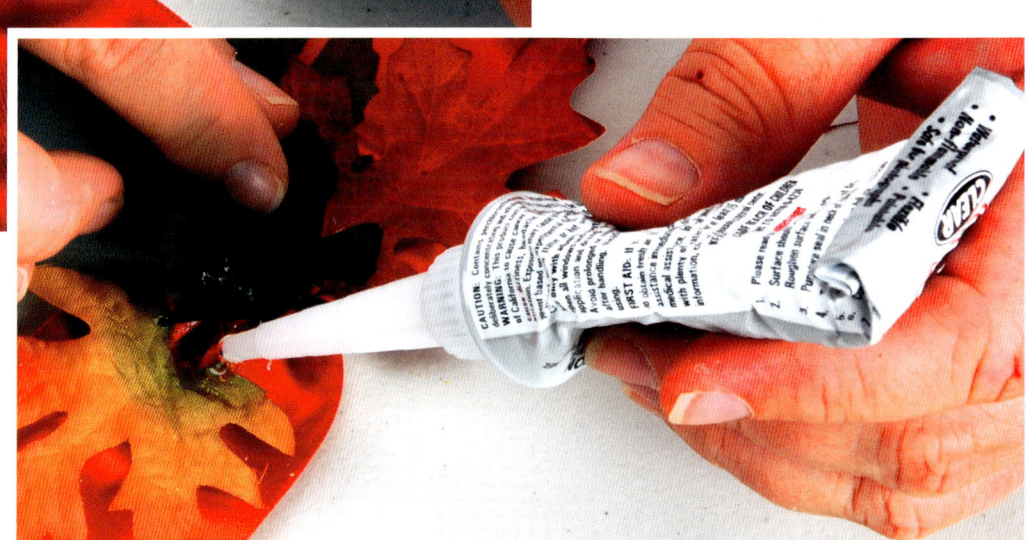

Attach the leaves to the ribbon with E6000 glue. Overlap the stems at the center of the ribbon, over the gathers.

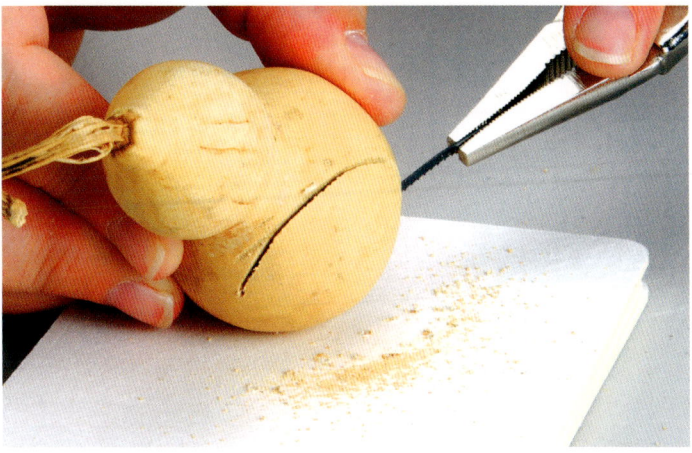

Cut off the back third of the mini-gourd belly.

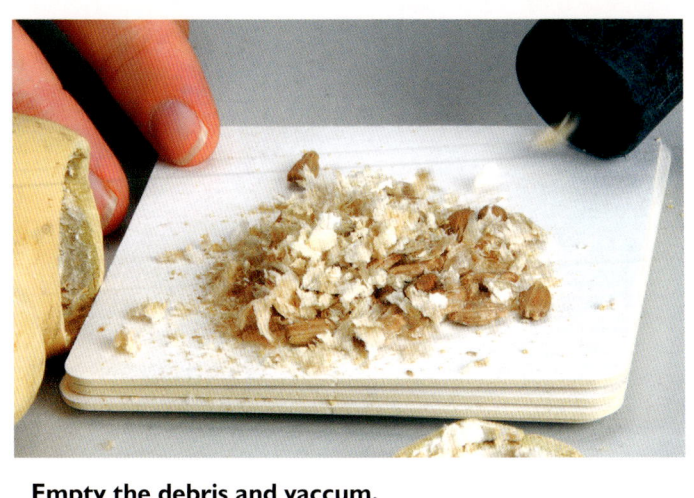

Empty the debris and vaccum.

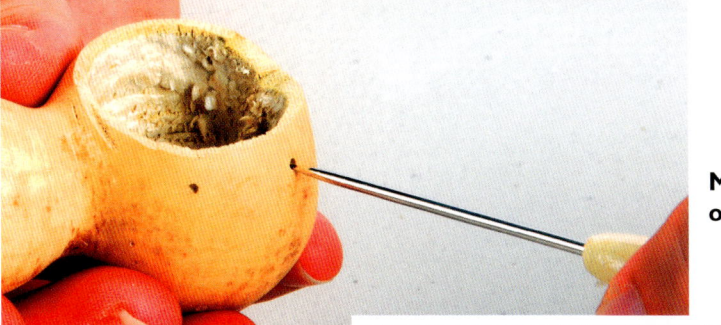

Make four sewing holes at the belly of the gourd, two on each side, using a darning needle.

Position the mini-gourd at the center, cut side down, onto the gathers and leaf stem bases.

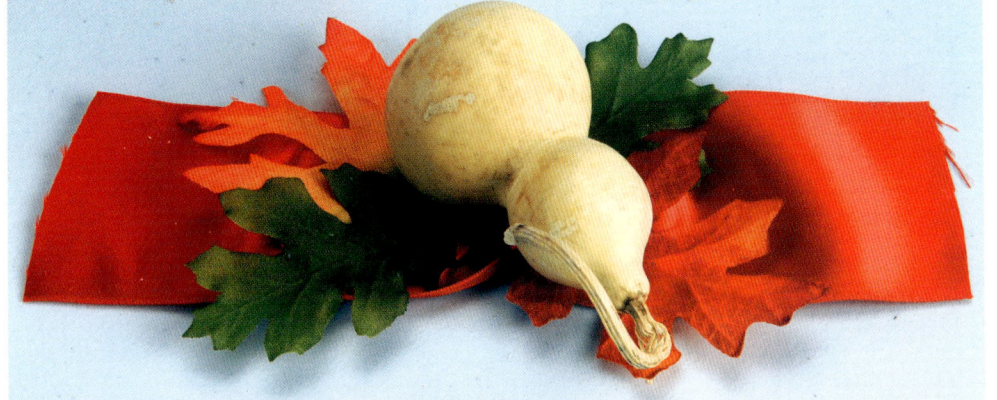

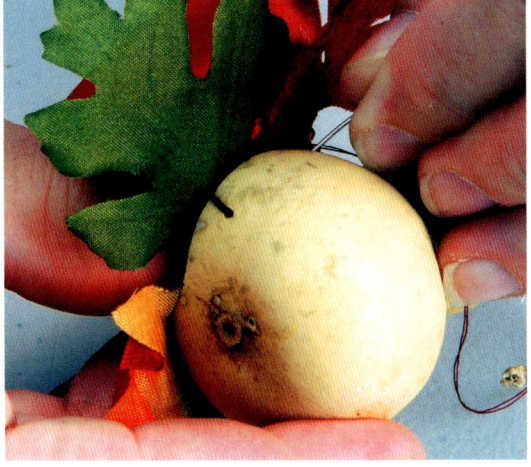

Turn the whole grouping over and sew the gourd to the ribbon, using the four holes punched into the gourd's belly.

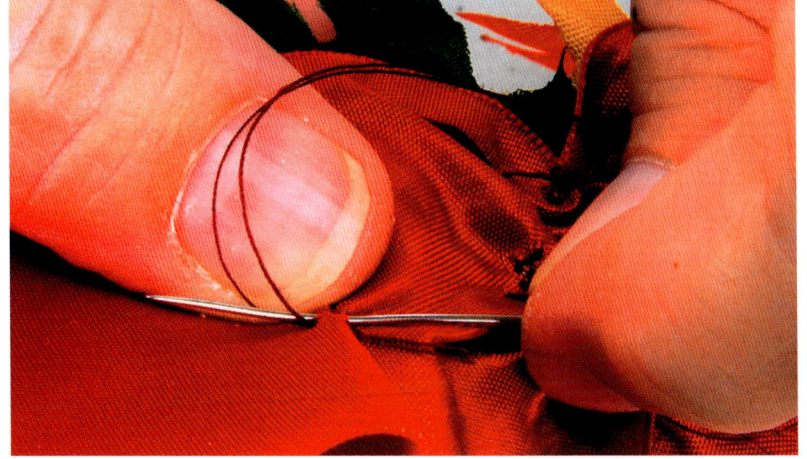

Fold each side of the ribbon back under a leaf by ½" and hold in position with a stitch.

43

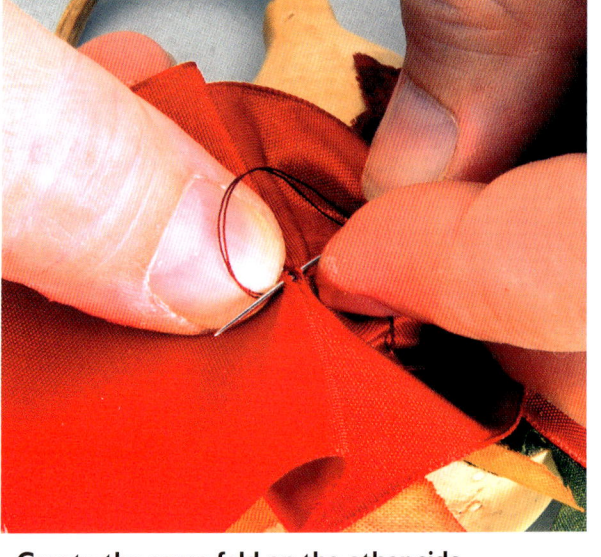

Create the same fold on the other side.

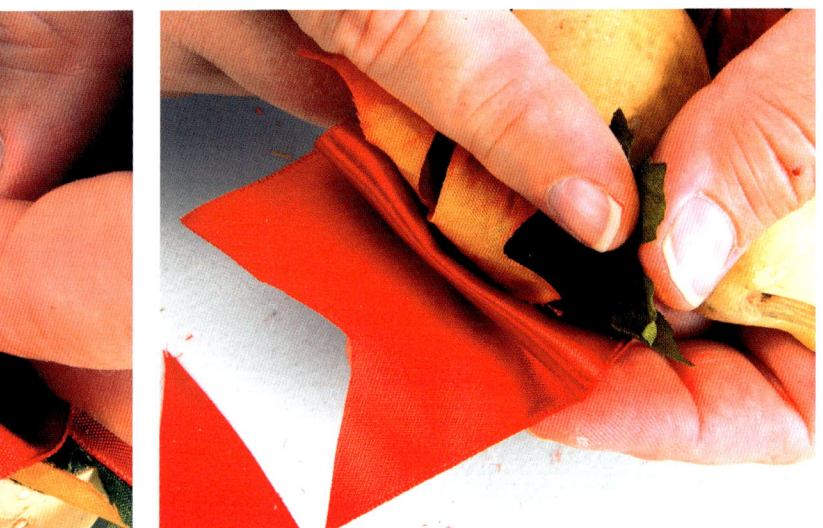

Trim both ends of the ribbon into points.

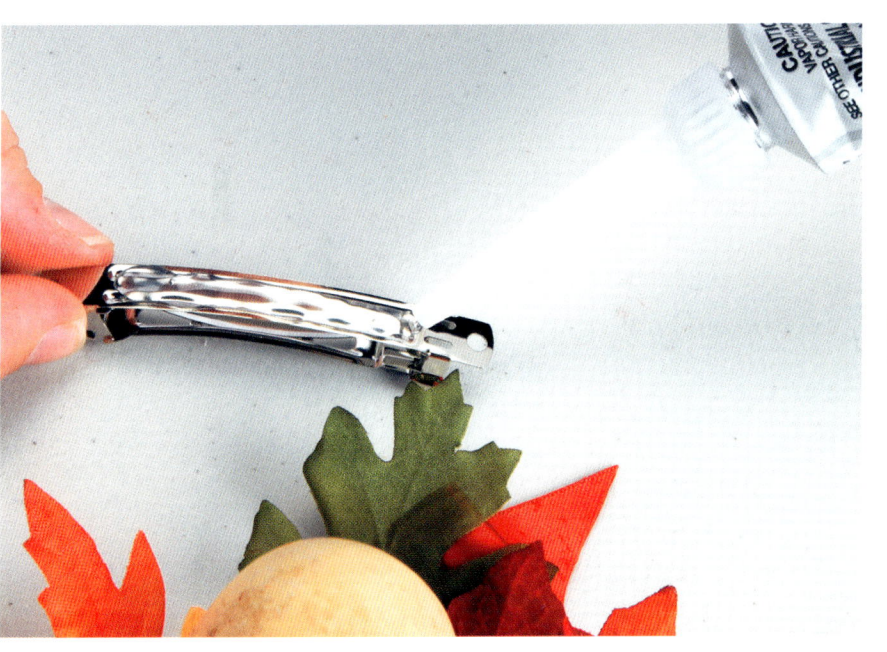

Run a line of **E6000** glue down the length of a barrette.

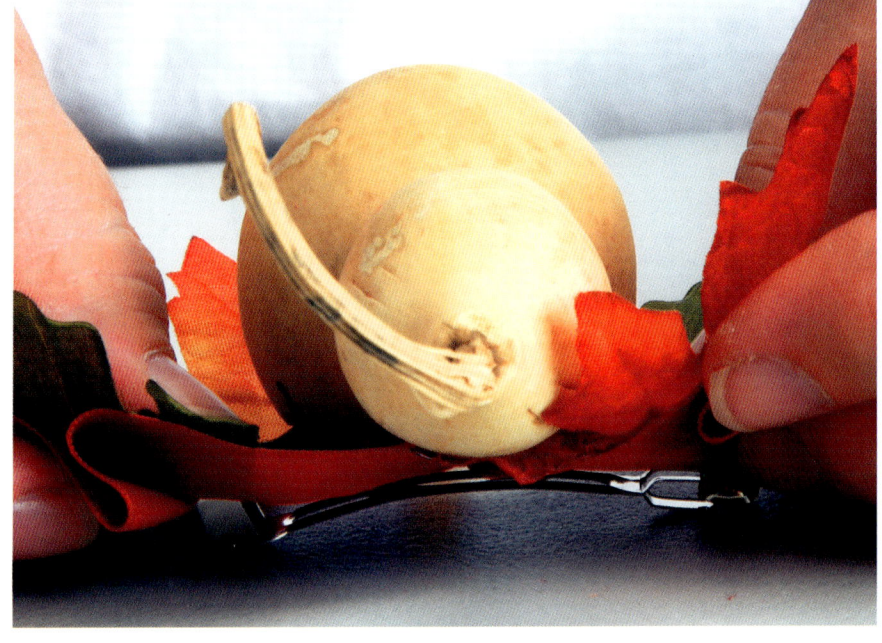

Center the grouping over the barrette and place it on the glue.

44

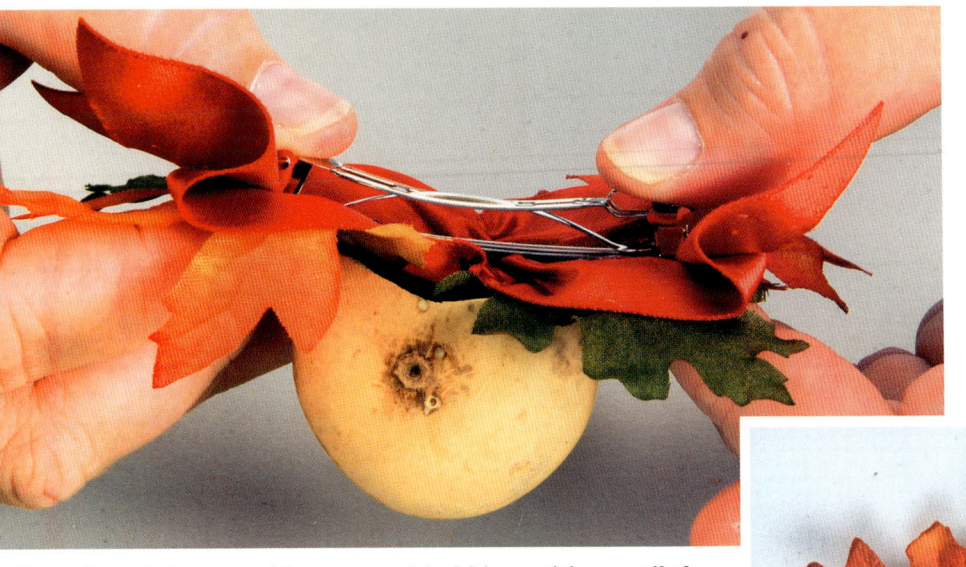

Turn the whole assembly over and hold in position until the glue sets.

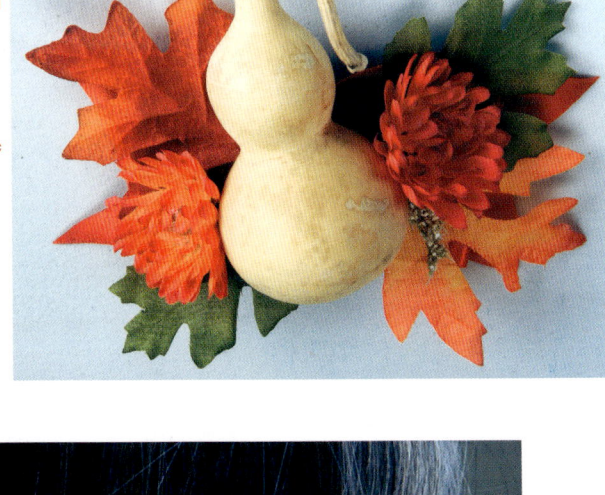

Add additional harvest details for interest.

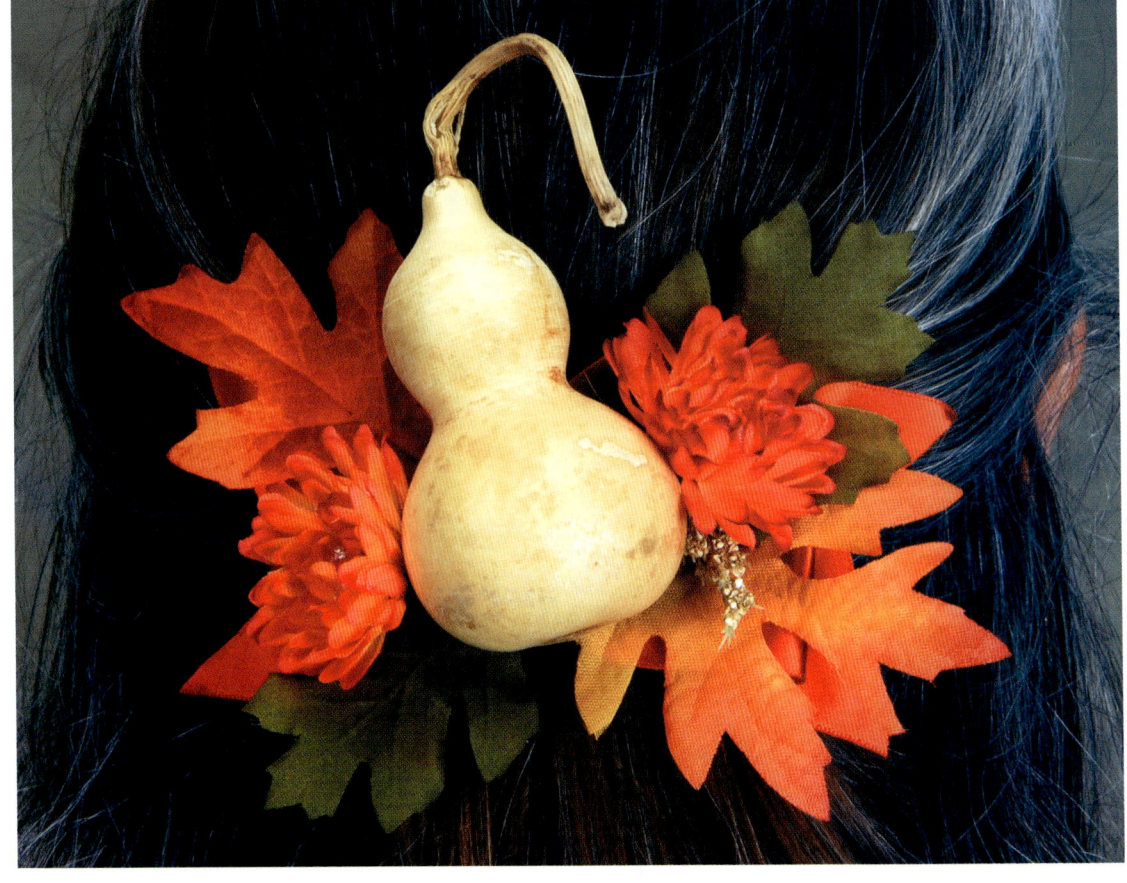

Pretty!

45

A Leafy Idea

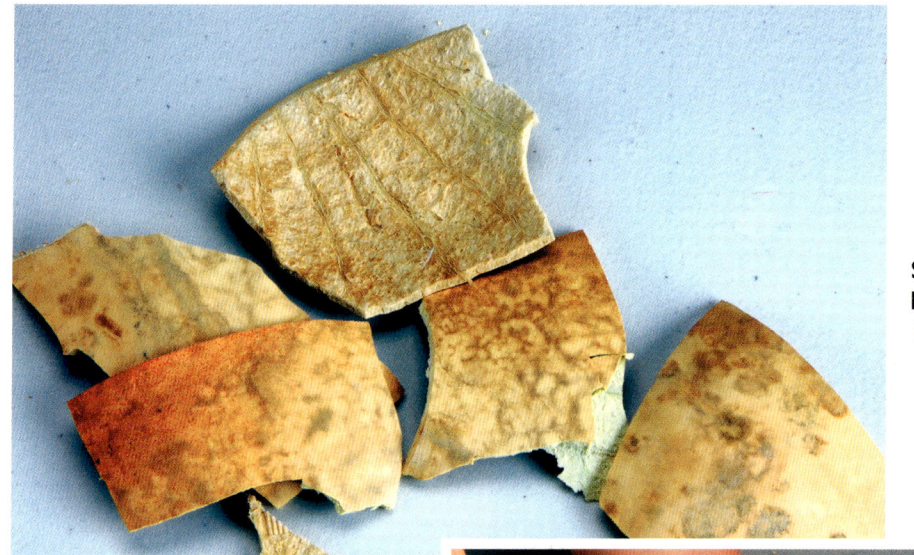

Since it's harvest time, let's try some leaves made from scraps. Find some 1-2" scraps.

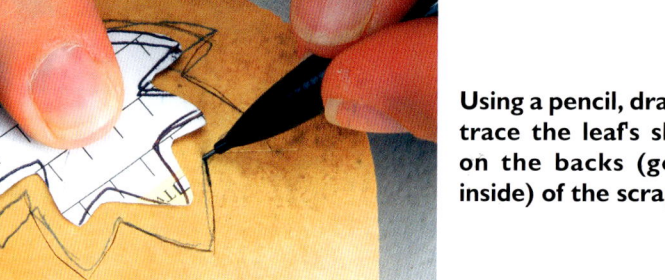

Using a pencil, draw or trace the leaf's shape on the backs (gourd inside) of the scraps.

Score the outlines lightly on the gourd surface, using a carpet knife.

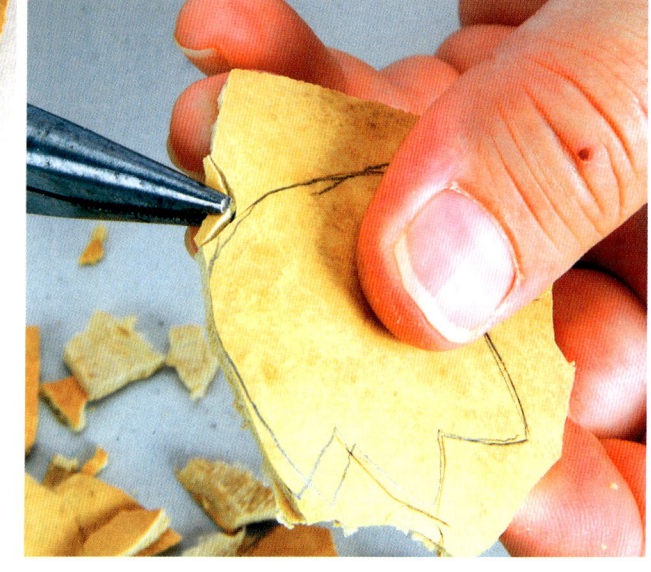

Using needle-nosed pliers, and taking small pinches at a time, squeeze-off pieces of the gourd up to the leaf outlines. Do not be too eager to get done fast because big pinches will only snap the gourd in the wrong places. Be karmic about this, and have some patience.

46

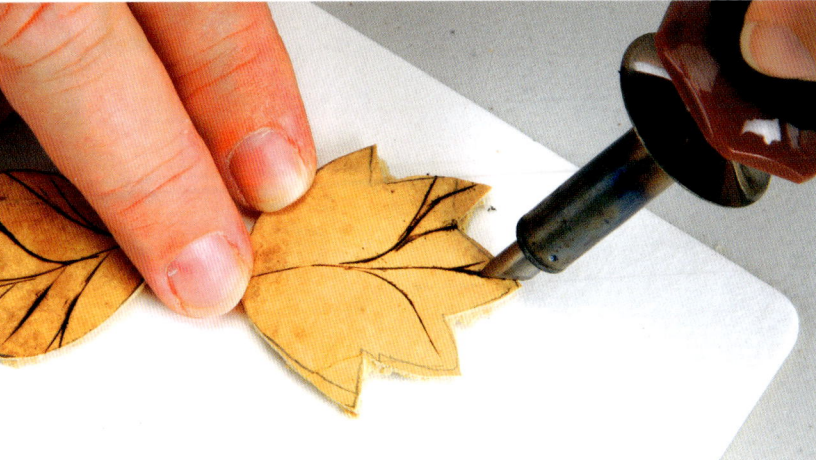

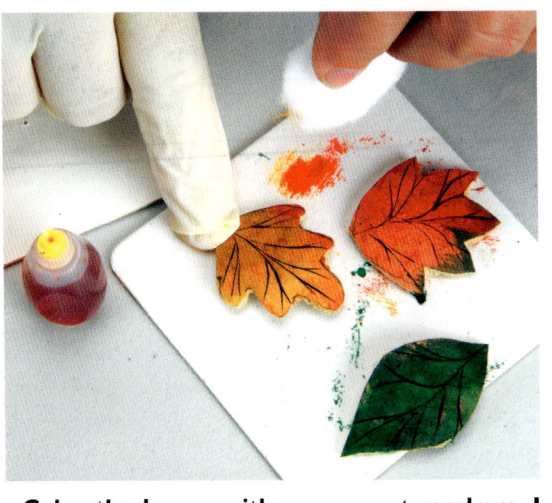

Using a woodburner with a chisel tip, make veins on the leaves. I like the chisel tip because it makes a clean line for texture.

Color the leaves with permanent markers. I am using cottonballs to apply food coloring. Either way, let these leaves dry thoroughly.

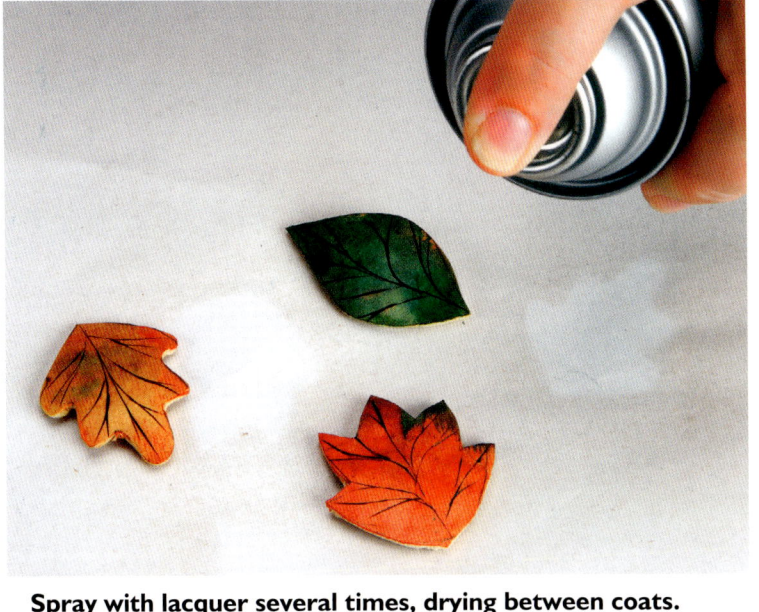

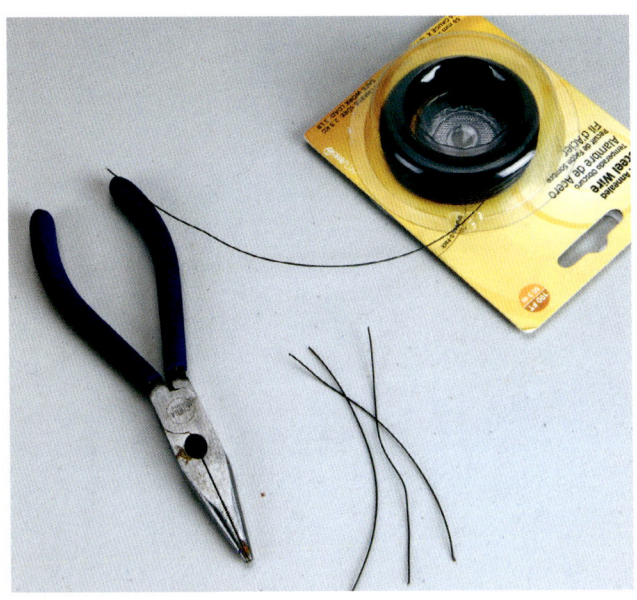

Spray with lacquer several times, drying between coats.

To attach the leaves to the barrette, cut three pieces of black 24-gauge wire, about 3" in length.

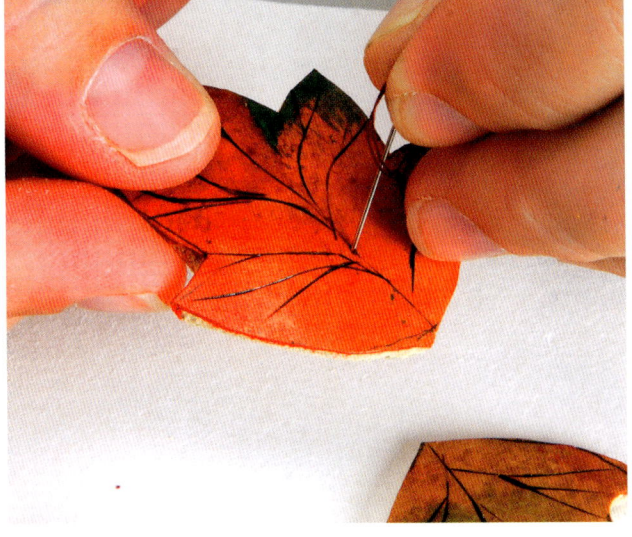

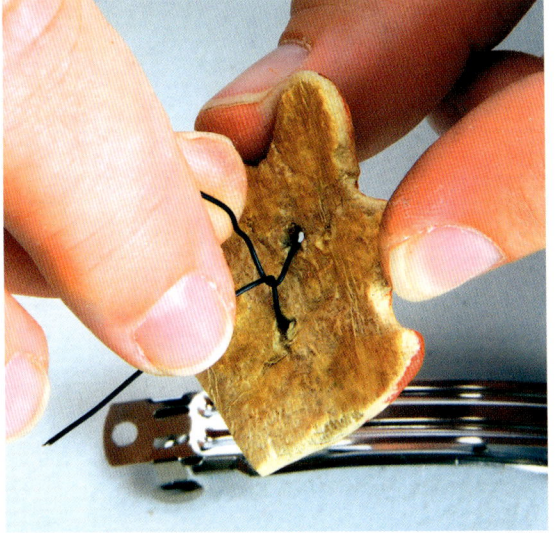

Make two needle holes along each of the leaves' main black, wood-burned vein.

Arrange the leaves in any order you wish, the center leaf overlapping the other two. Take each leaf, push the wire ends through the holes and twist.

47

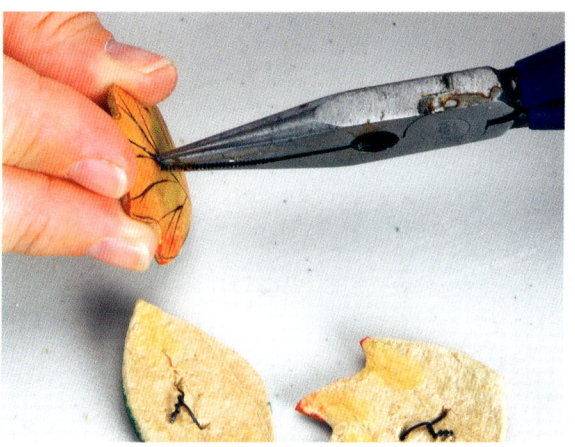

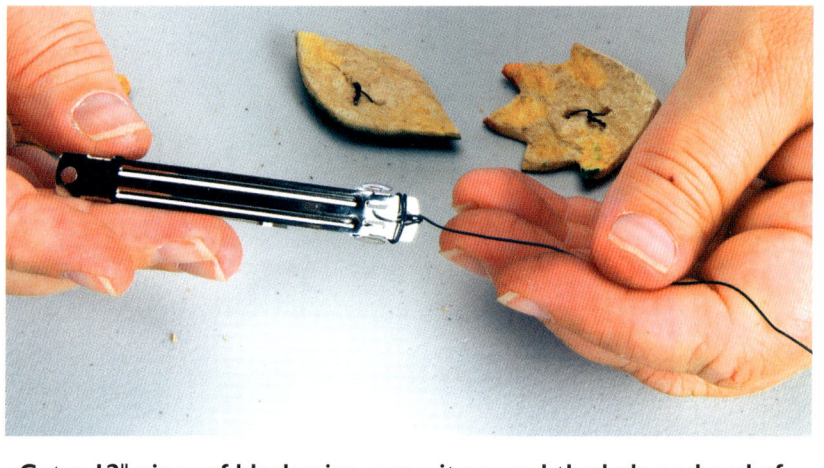

At the back of each leaf, bend down the twisted wire. On the front of each leaf, crimp the wire.

Cut a 12" piece of black wire, wrap it around the hole and end of one side of the barrette.

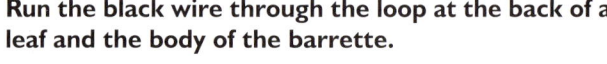

Run the black wire through the loop at the back of a leaf and the body of the barrette.

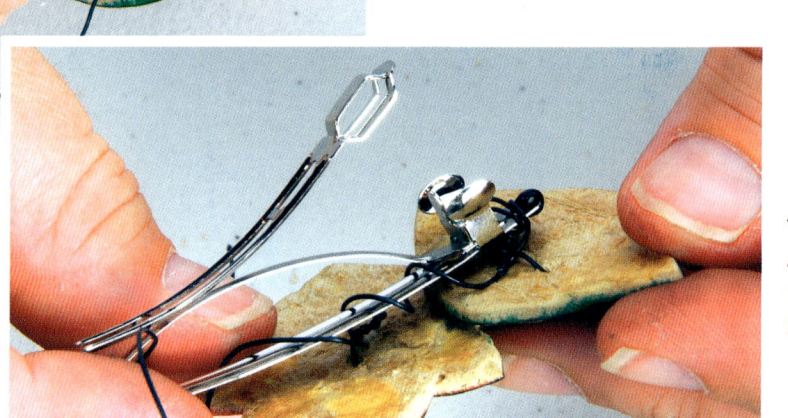

Wrap the black wire around and catch the next leaf; repeat the procedure.

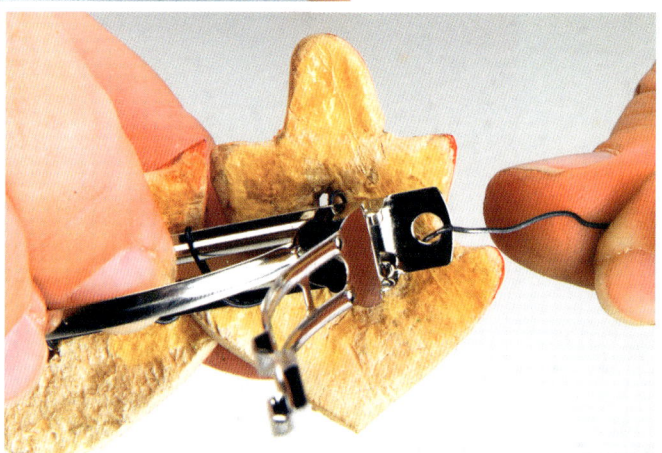

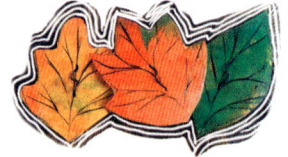

Keep going for the third leaf, and end at the barrette hole on the other side.

48

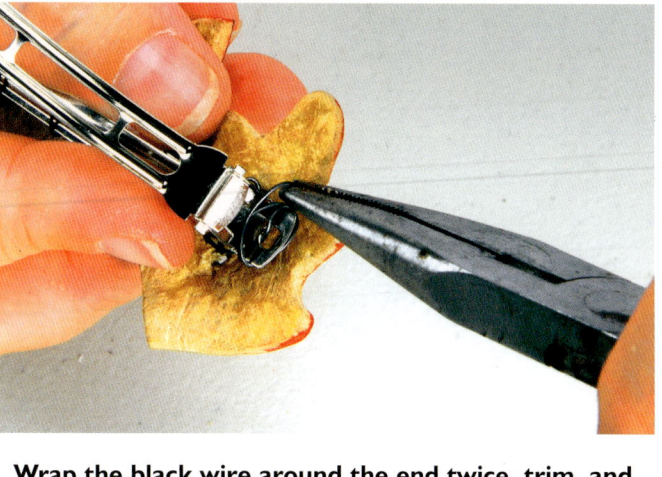

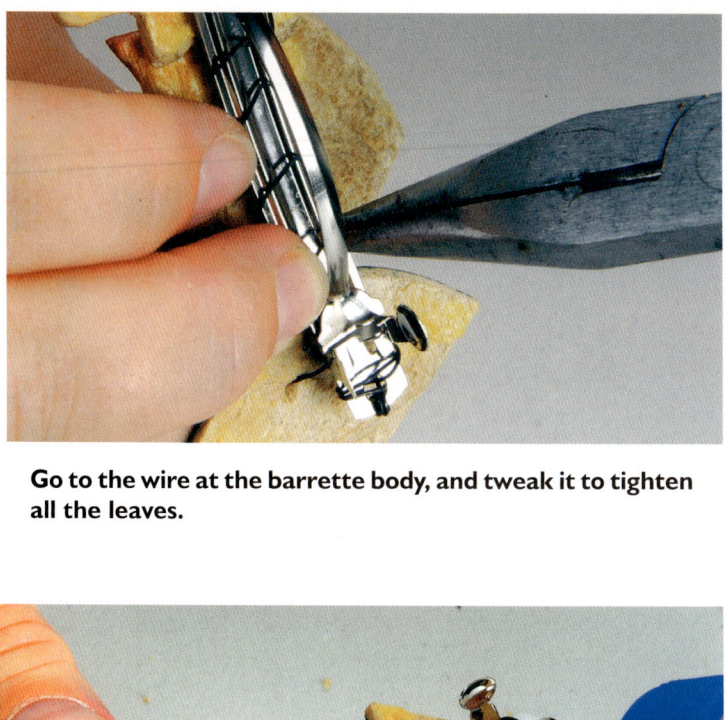

Wrap the black wire around the end twice, trim, and tuck the end away.

Go to the wire at the barrette body, and tweak it to tighten all the leaves.

As added insurance, place a dot of wood glue at the seams where the leaves meet. *NOTE: If using thick gourd scraps, this step may not be necessary.*

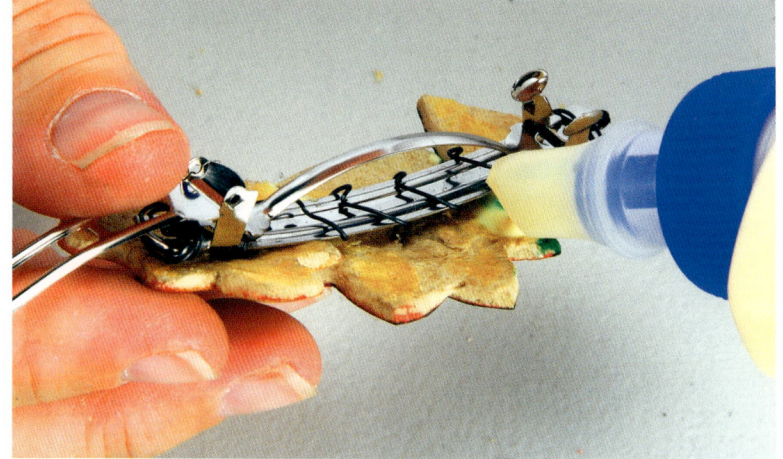

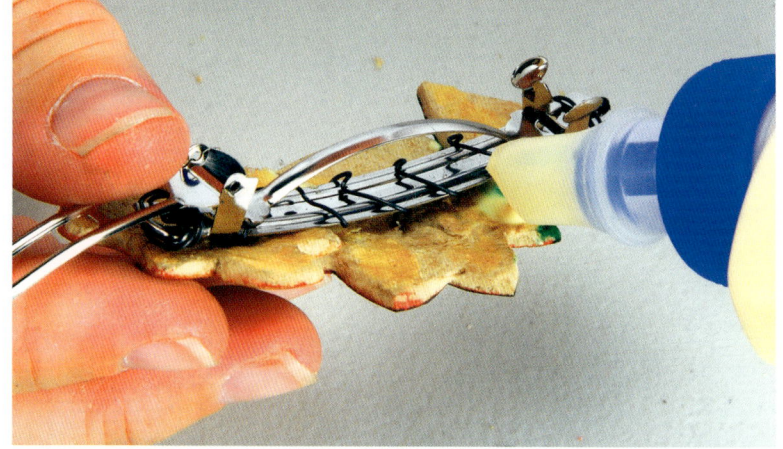

Another successful gourd story!

49

Chapter Five:

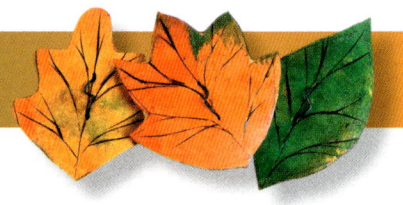

Thinking Caps

This is the secret! This is how I come up with all the "gourdiness" you have read about in my books. My personal thinking cap was made years ago when I was in the garage and was playing with the scrap top of a gourd I had used to make a bowl. A little wire, some costume jewelry, ribbon, imagination, and a thinking cap can come to life.

However, two issues need to be considered while having fun with this project: balance and stability. Make sure the cap is not overly weighted to one side or has a center of gravity high over the cap because it will never stay on your head, no matter how tightly it's tied.

Let's start thinking!

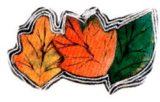

Full Cap: ◇◇

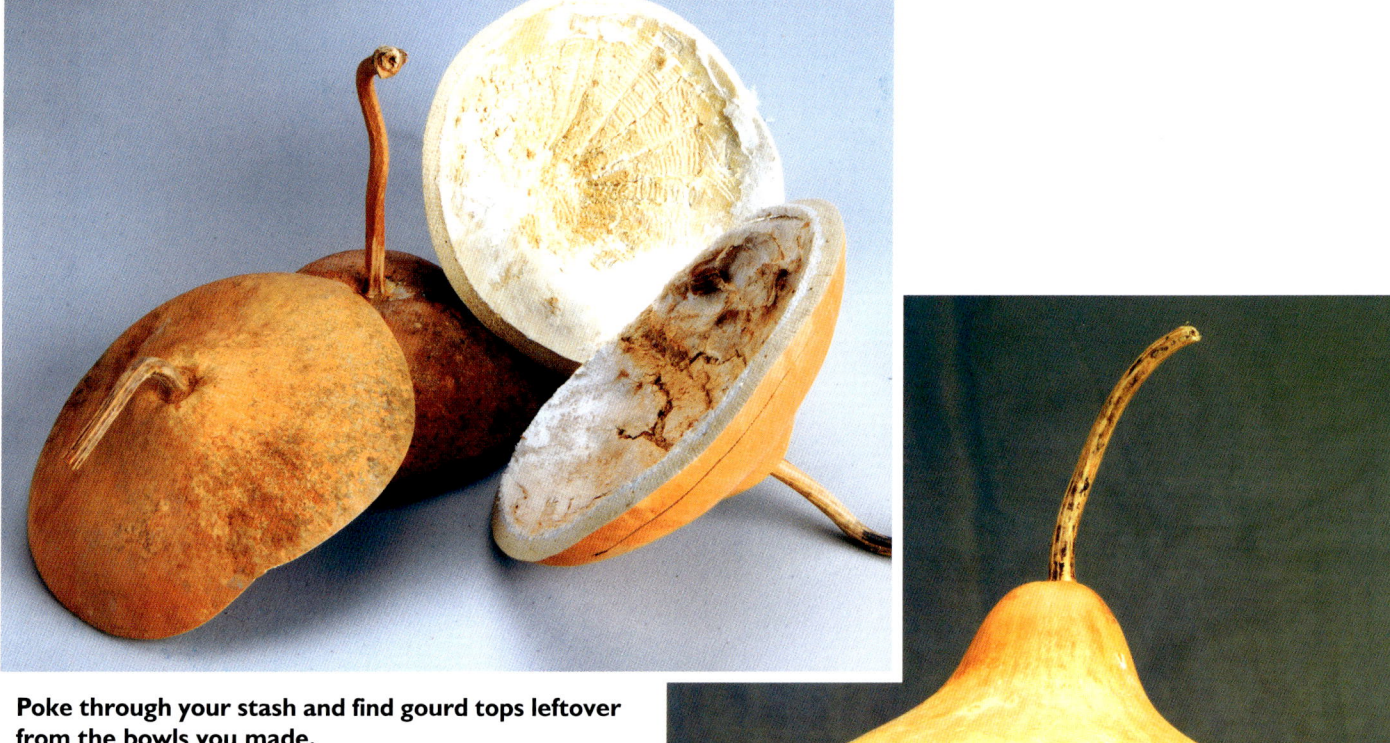

Poke through your stash and find gourd tops leftover from the bowls you made.

Start with one you particularly like, one that cradles your head nicely.

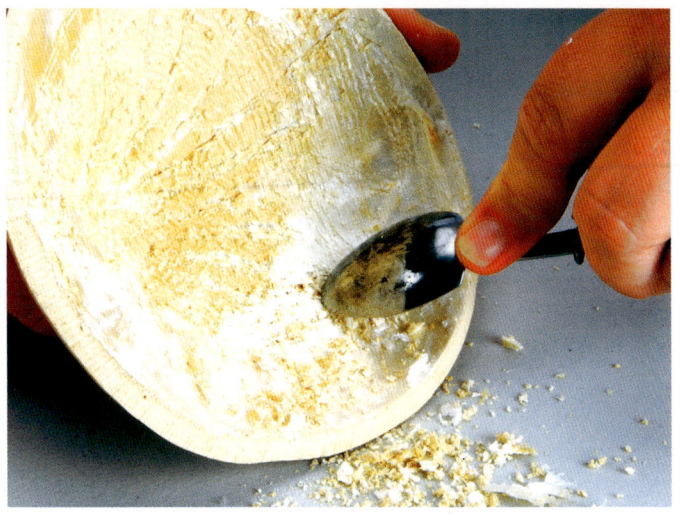

Turn it over to clean the underside by scraping the pith loose from the gourd wall...

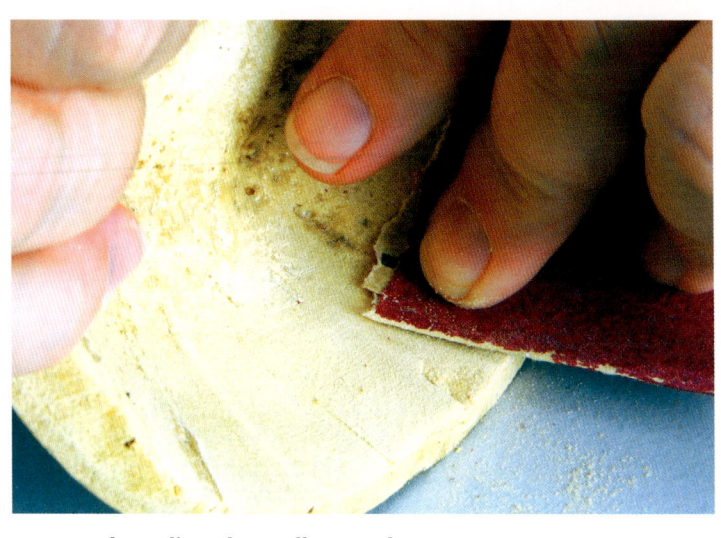

...and sanding the wall smooth.

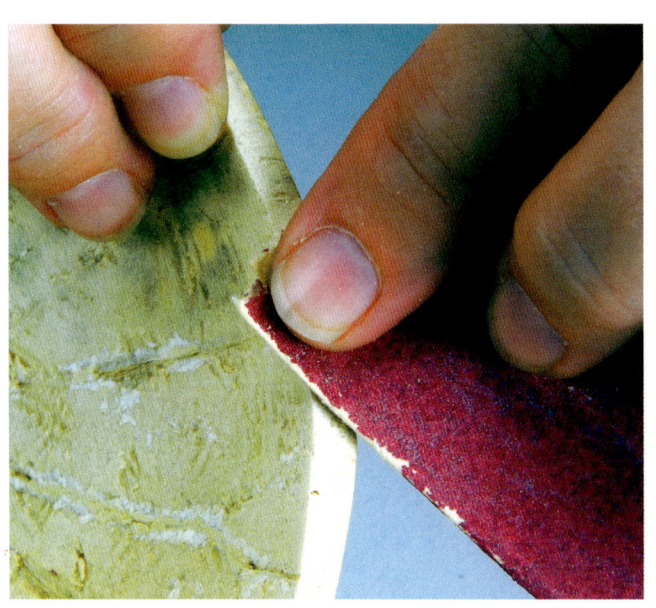

Sand the edges smooth.

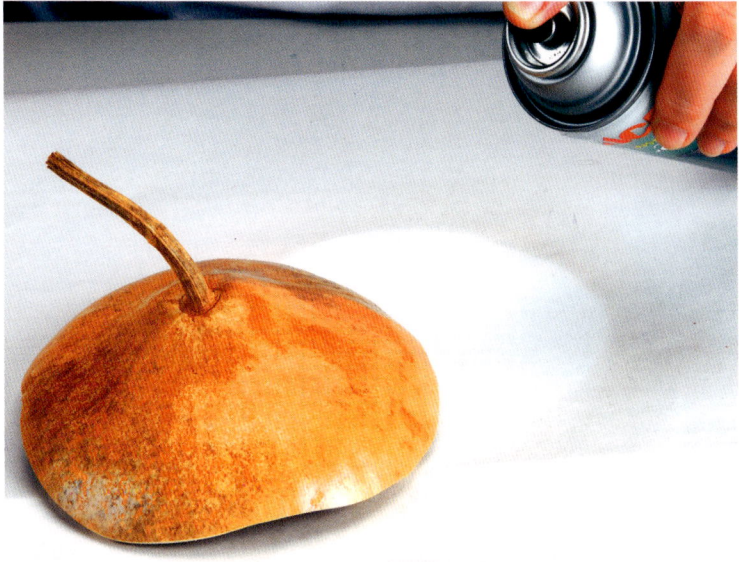

Spray the outside of the gourd top with lacquer or brush on a coat of polyurethane. I like several coats for even coverage. Let dry.

While the top is drying, select an odd number of costume jewelry pieces, mini-gourds, or machine parts.

Using a drill, make six holes into the gourd top at random places. The randomness of these holes is the genius of a gourd thinking cap. If you align them too obviously, the karma goes bad. Just so you know.

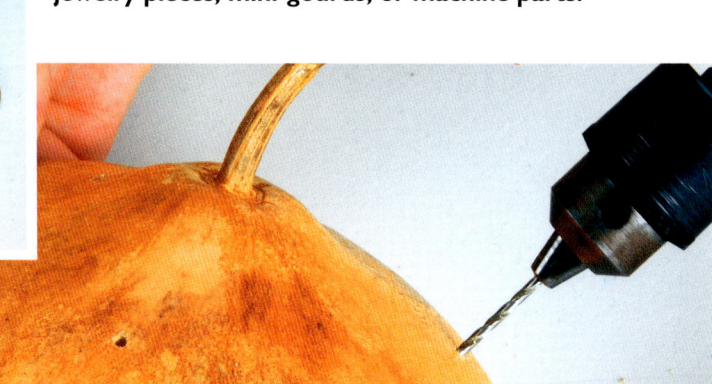

51

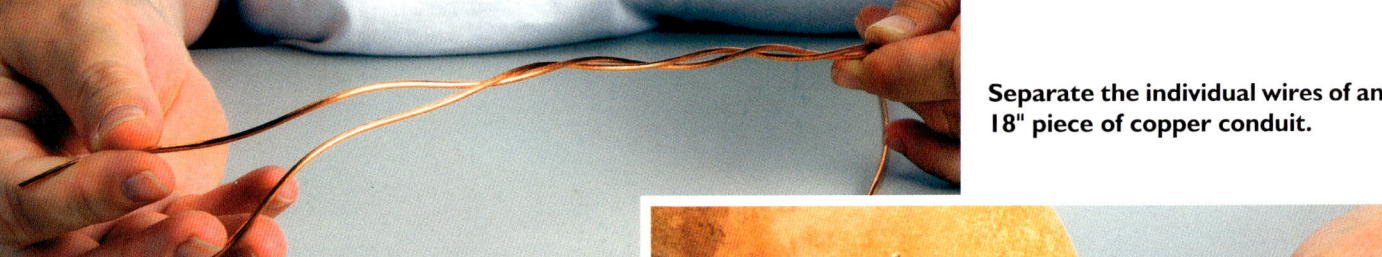

Separate the individual wires of an 18" piece of copper conduit.

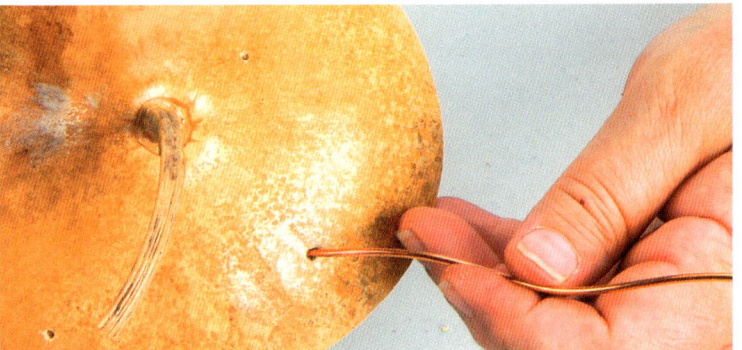

Put the end of one piece into a hole, leaving a 6" tail.

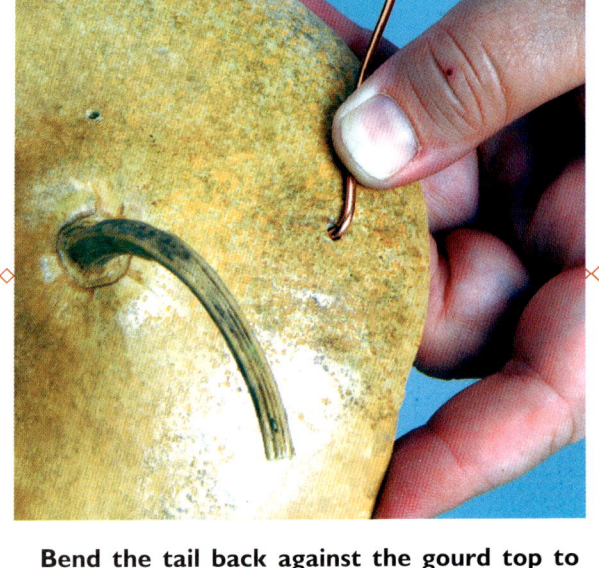

Bend the tail back against the gourd top to anchor it in place.

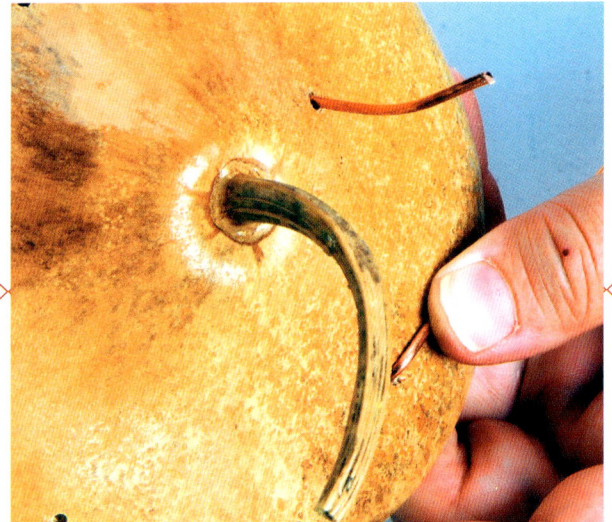

Put the opposite end of the wire into, and out of, the nearest hole.

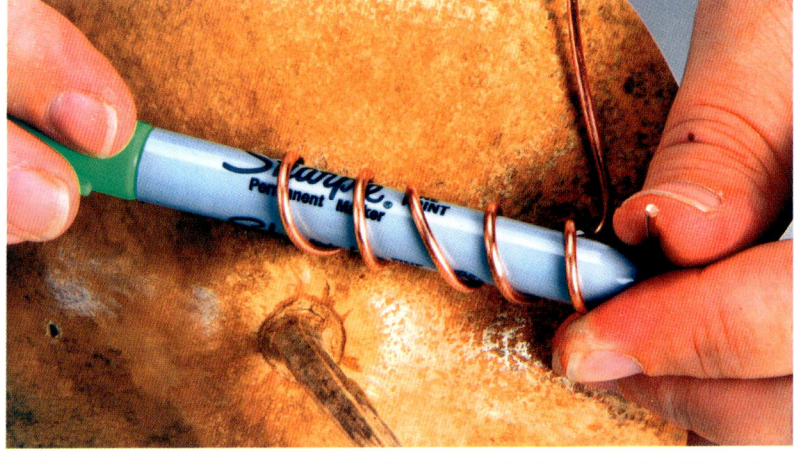

Twirl the wire coming out of the second hole around a Sharpie or dowel.

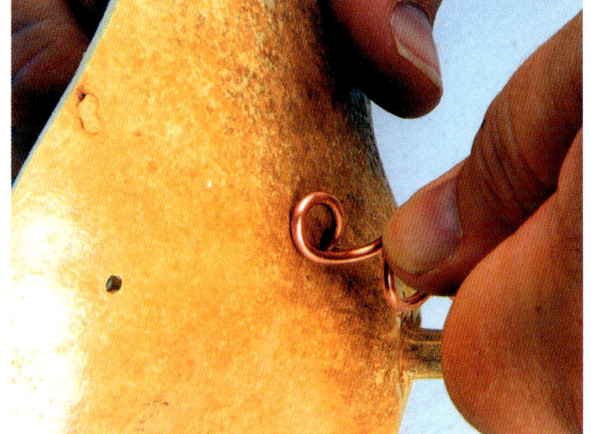

Spin the newly-made spiral around so that it corkscrews against the gourd and tightens it.

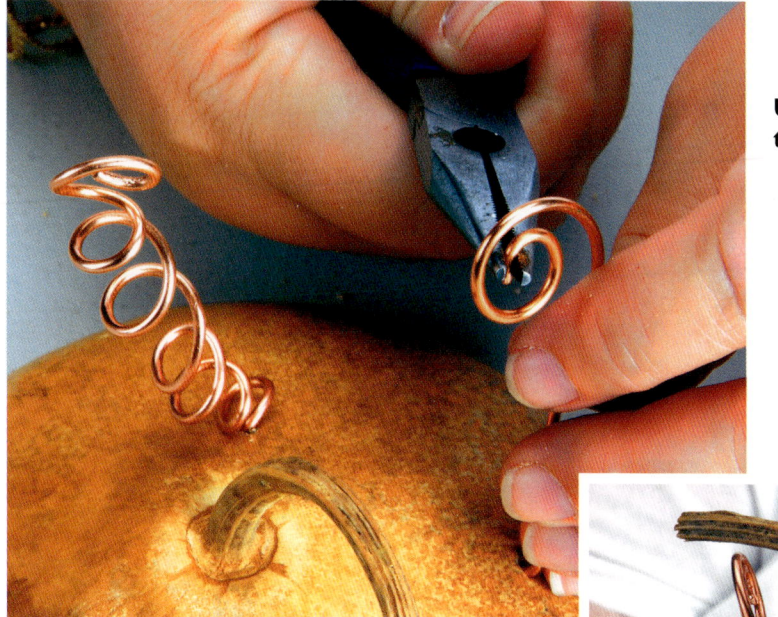

Use needle-nosed pliers and curl both ends of the wire to make hooks.

Hang pieces of costume jewelry or a gourd from the curled wire hooks.

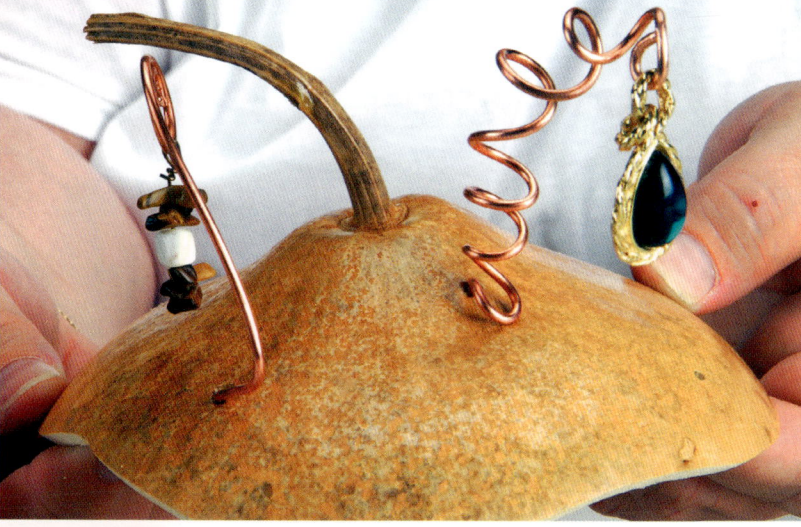

Squeeze the hooks closed.

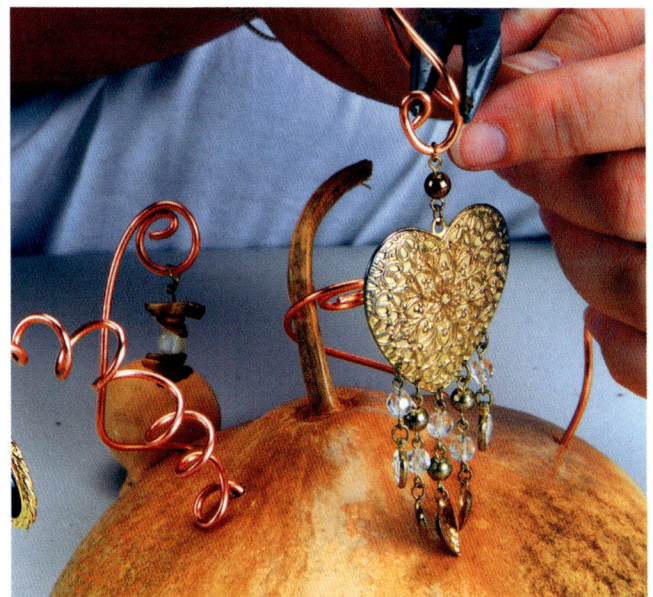

Do another piece of wire and hang more of the costume jewelry you selected earlier.

Continue with the last wire in the last set of holes.

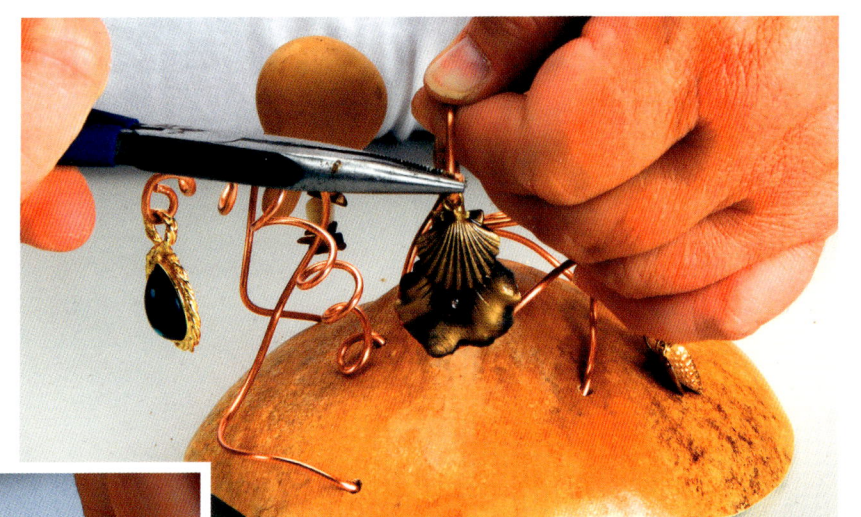

If you find that a wire seems loose, turn the gourd top over and locate the affected wire underneath. Clamp the wire with the pliers and turn. The turning will take up any slack in the wire and tighten the length overall.

Once you have finished the thinking capabilities of the cap, check it for balance so that one side is not heavier than the other. Drill holes at the sides of the top for ties.

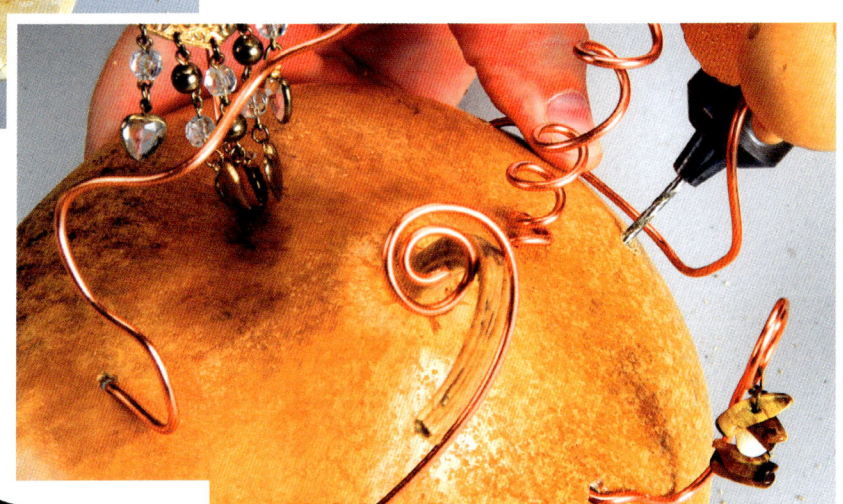

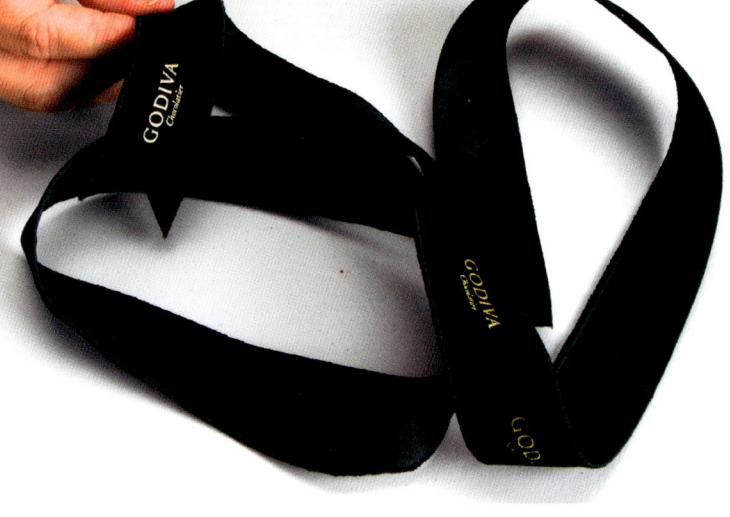

For ties, choose a wide ribbon, perhaps 2½-3" wide and 5' long. The width acts as a stabilizer for the cap. A thin ribbon just does not have enough body to keep the cap from tipping from one side to another.

54

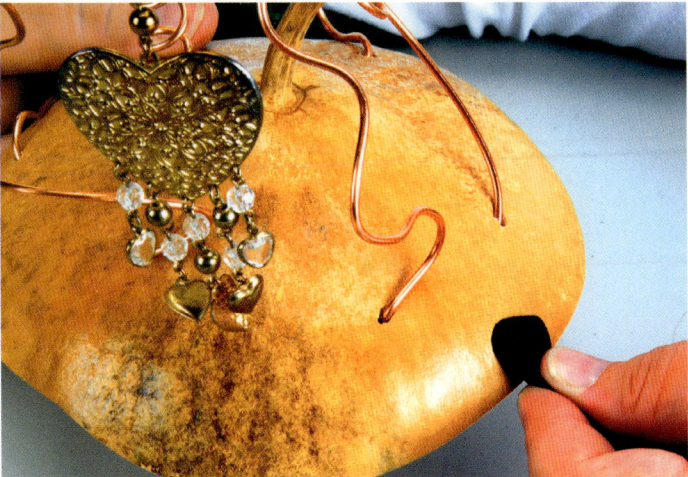
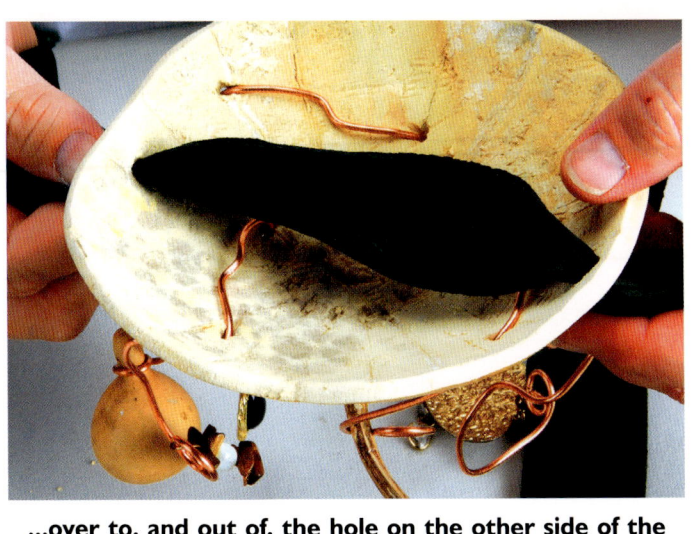

Take one end into the hole on one side of the cap...

...over to, and out of, the hole on the other side of the cap.

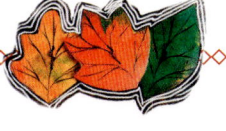

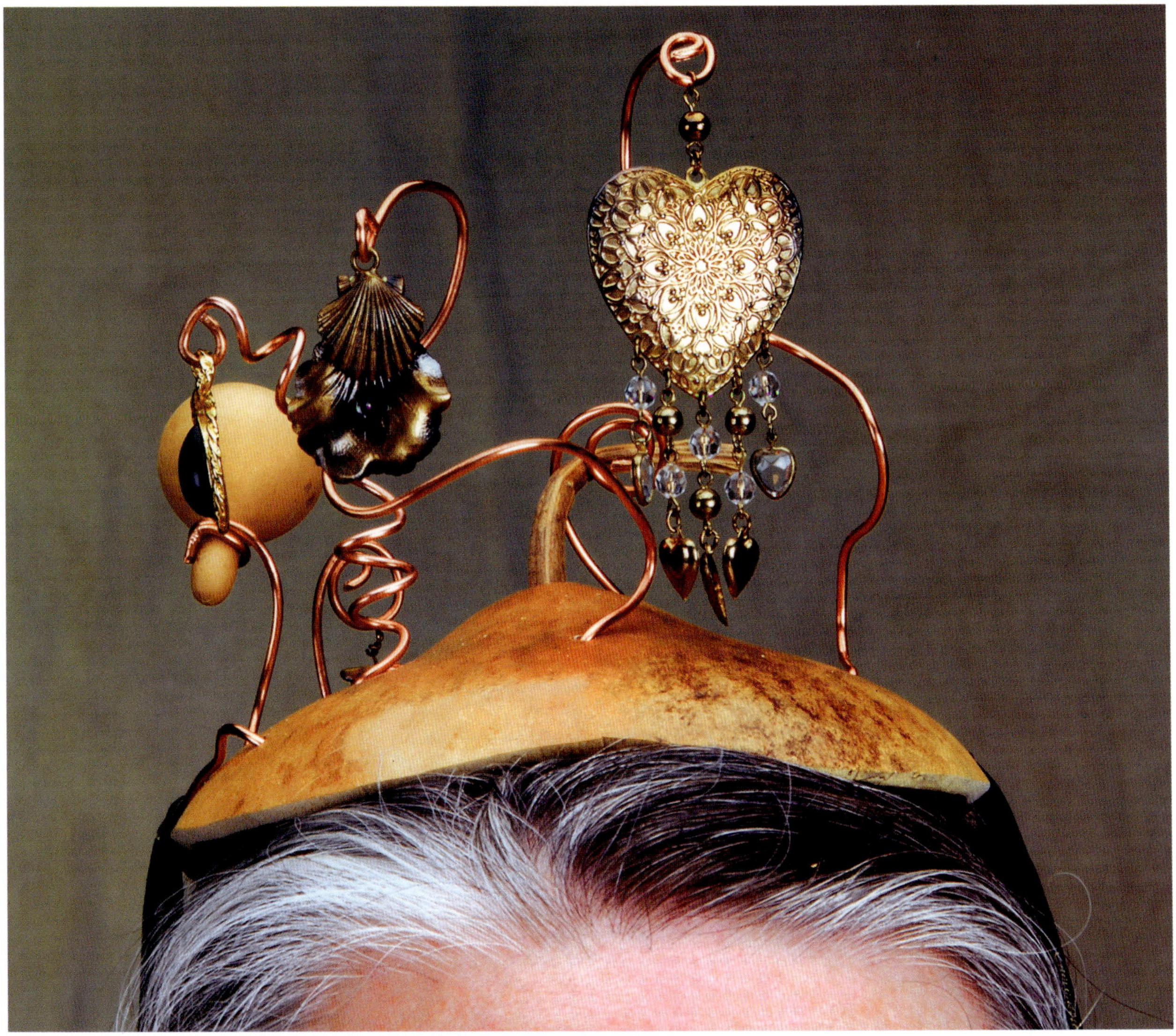

Your head will push against and adjust the interior area of ribbon, and the ties will hold the whole affair securely on the head.

55

Light Bulb: ◇◇◇

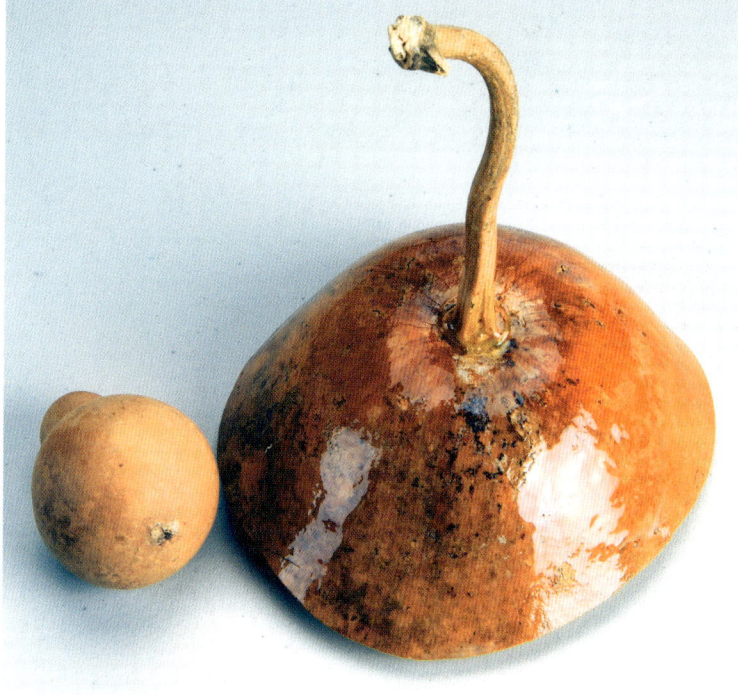

A similar gourd thinking cap uses a smaller gourd top and a small bottleneck gourd to make a light bulb thinking cap.

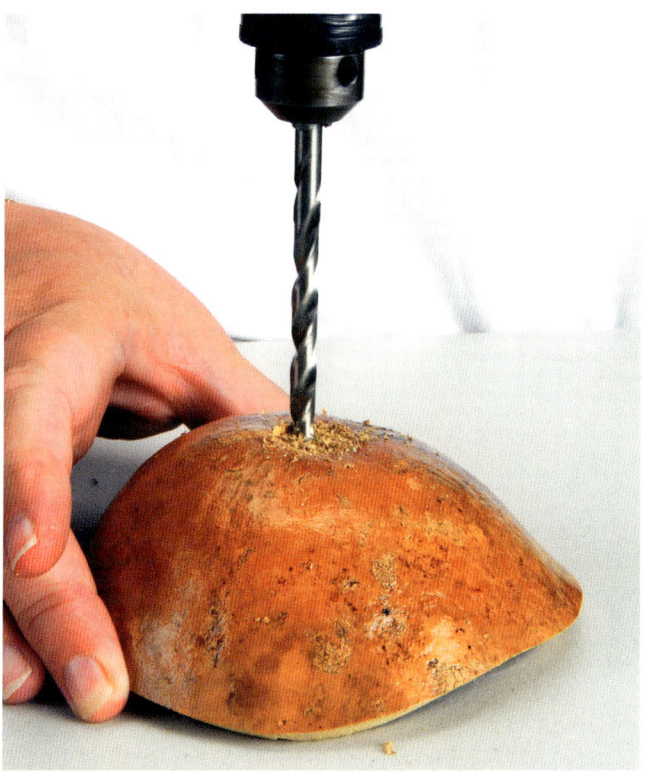

Clean and prepare the gourd top as we did earlier except this time, drill a hole into the stem end of the gourd top.

Make sure the hole is big enough to fit a small coiled-metal spring.

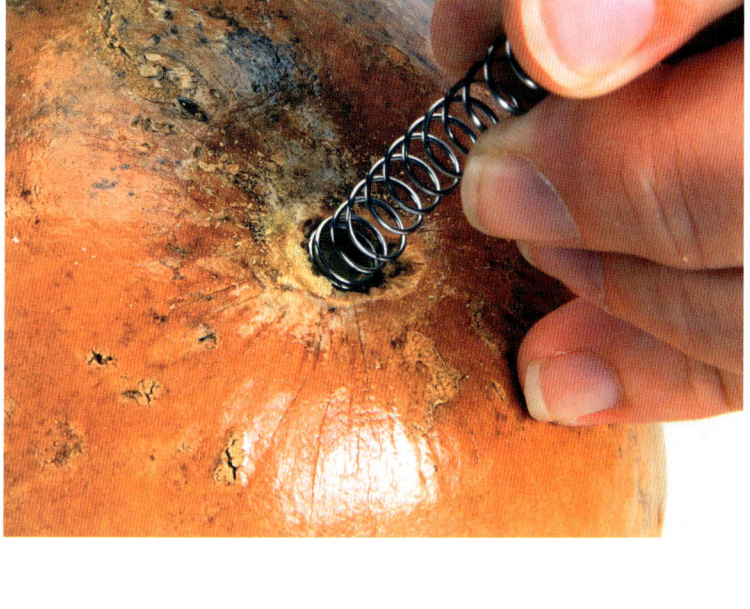

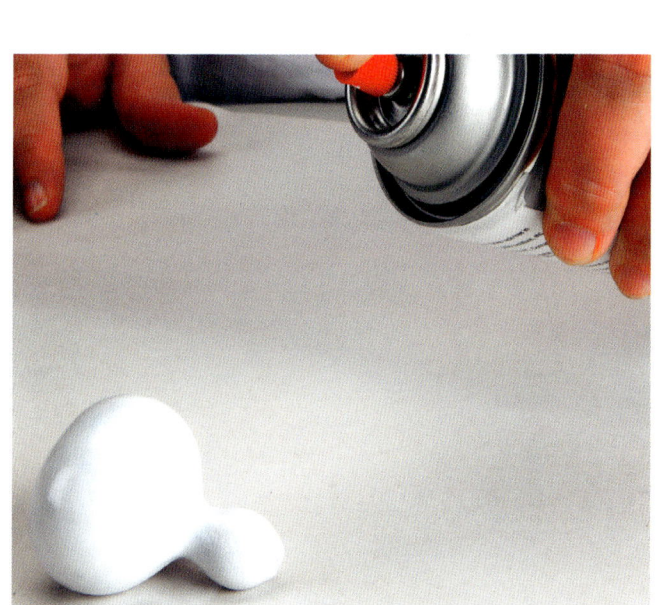

Paint the belly and neck of the small bottleneck gourd a bright white-yellow color.

56

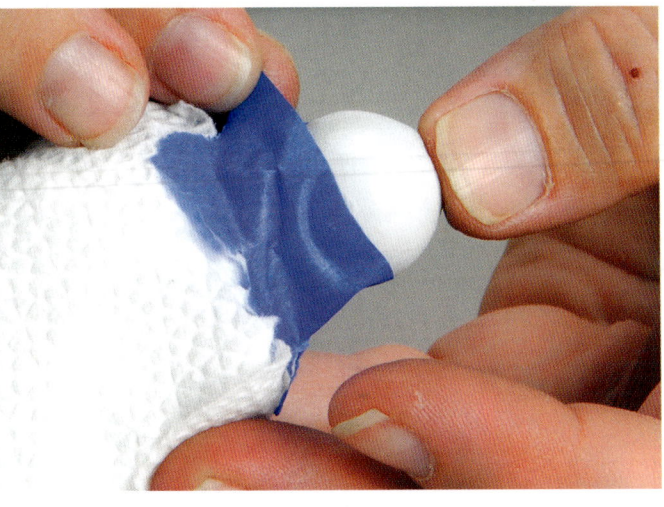

When it is dry, wrap a piece of painter's tape and paper towel around the gourd, ¾" from the end. This will be a mask for future spray paint.

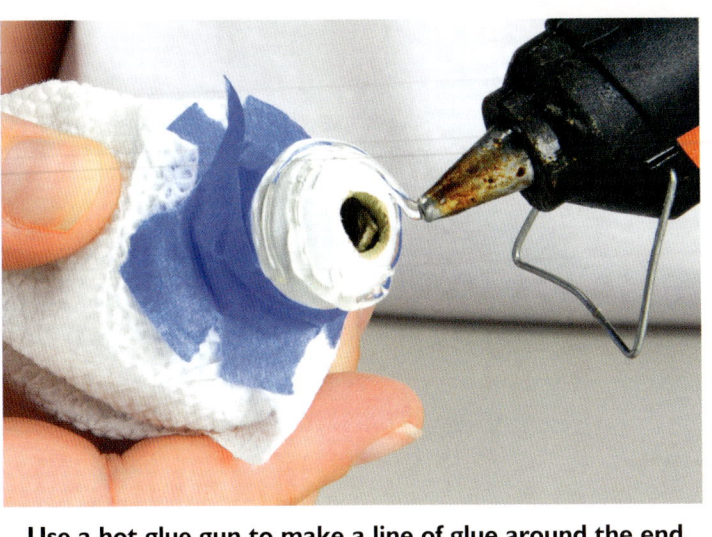

Use a hot glue gun to make a line of glue around the end in a spiral. Let dry.

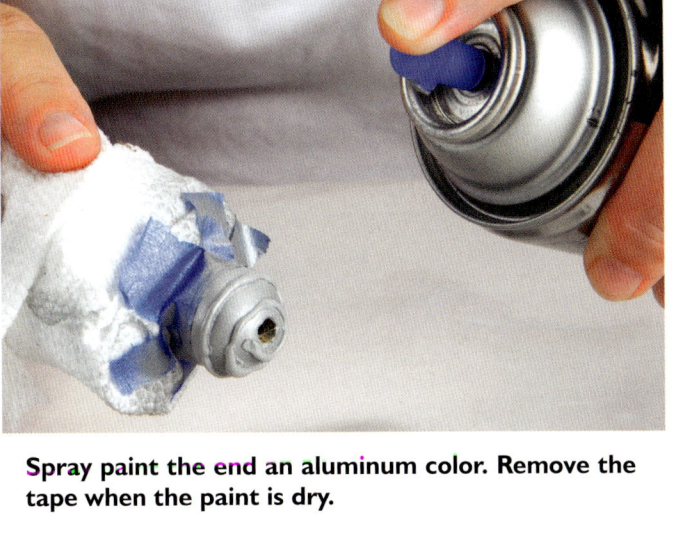

Spray paint the end an aluminum color. Remove the tape when the paint is dry.

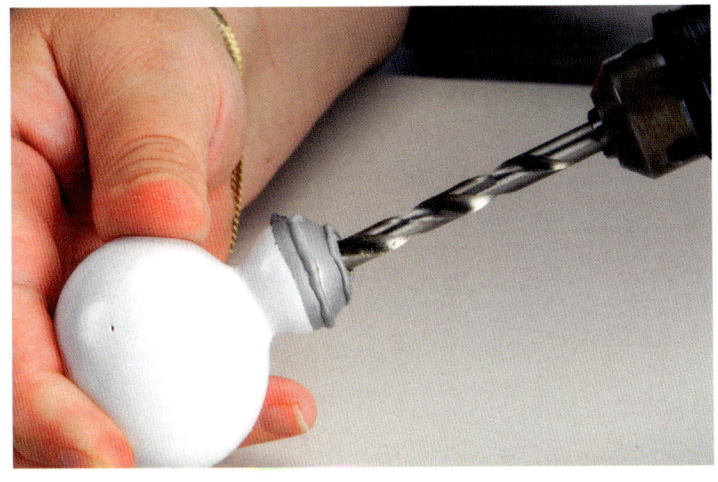

Drill a hole into the aluminum-colored end of the gourd.

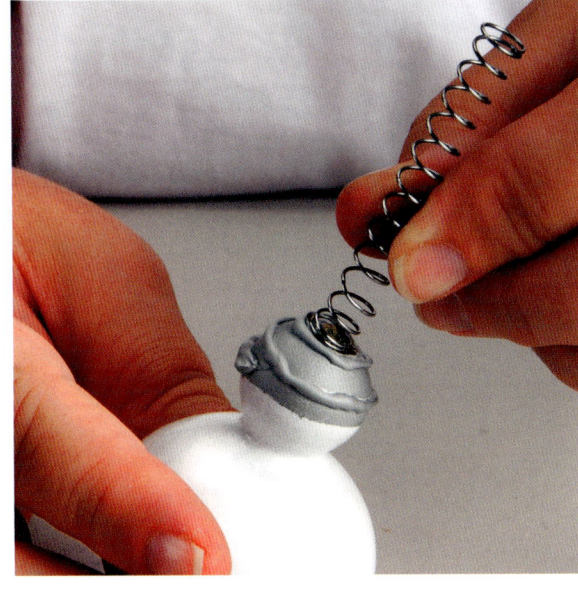

Using a hot glue gun, bond an 11/16" x 2½" spring to the end, and let cool.

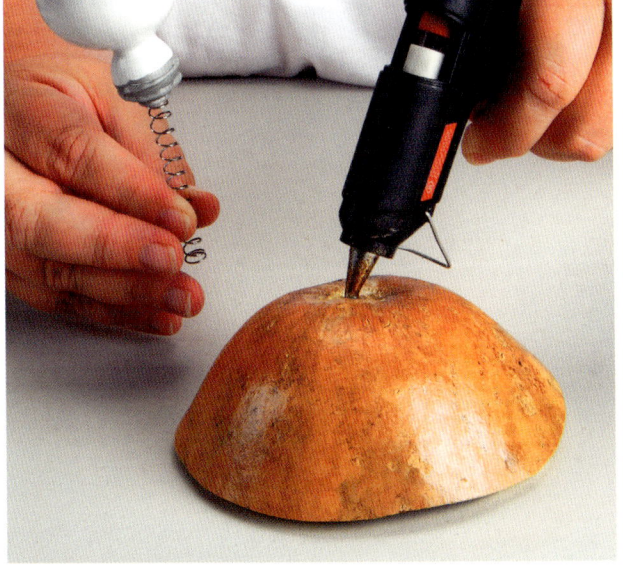

Squeeze the same hot glue into the stem hole made in the gourd top...

57

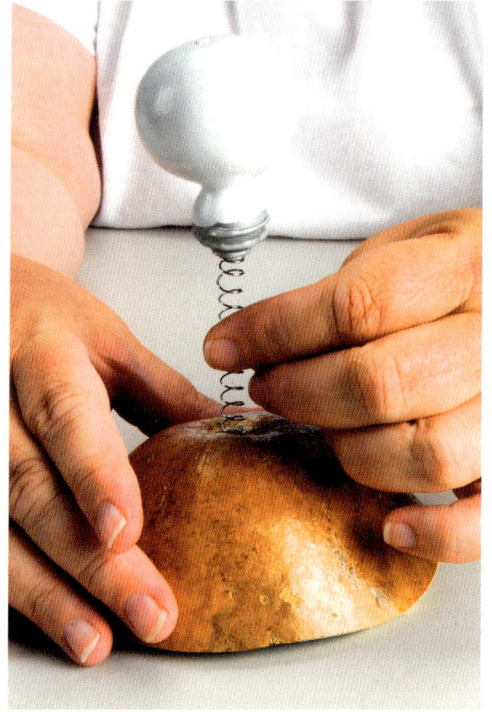
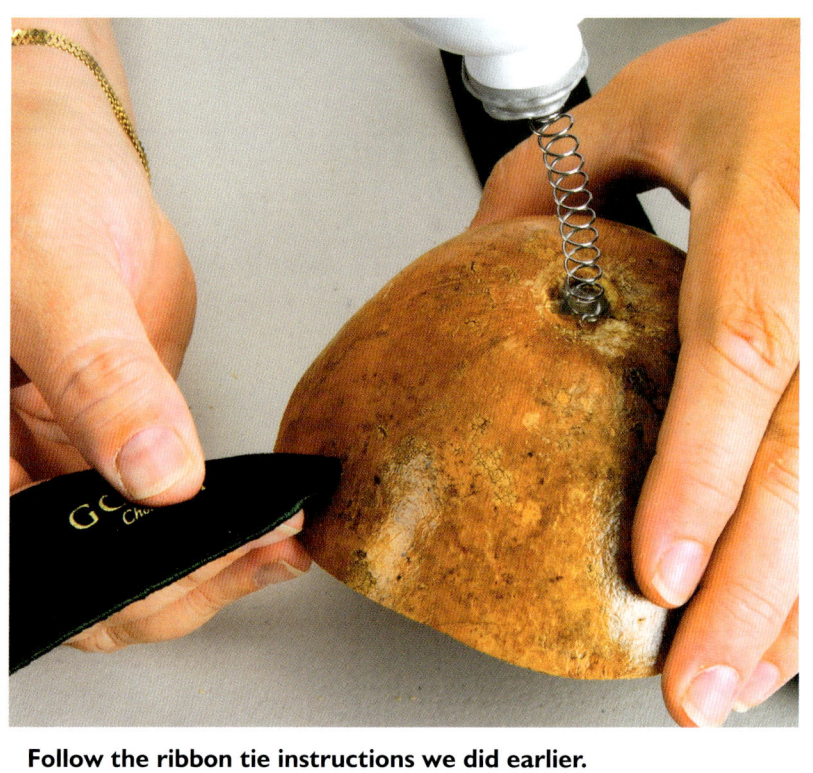

...and insert the spring with the light bulb. Let cool.

Follow the ribbon tie instructions we did earlier.

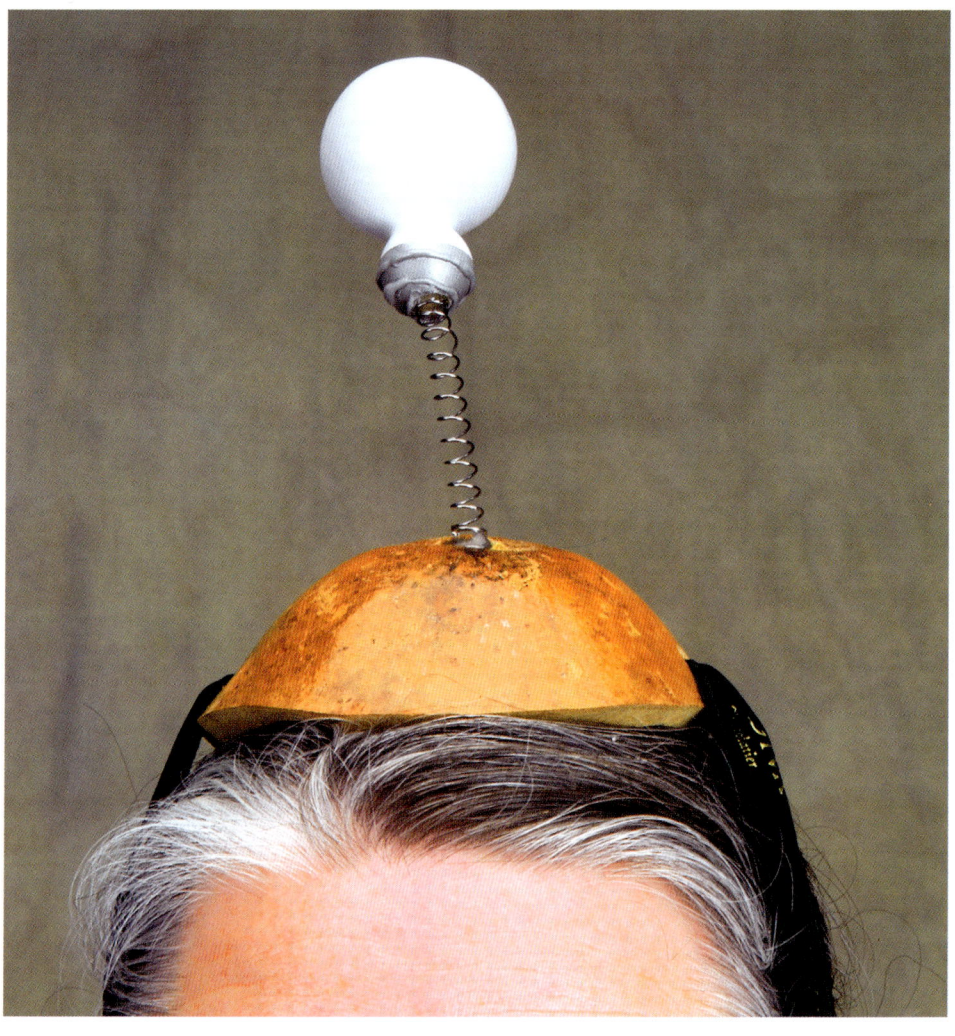

MmMmmm, thinking about more ideas...like, what will my editor to let me do next?

Concluding Words

Each one of these projects can be expanded to a book by themselves! Take the basics shown and use your imagination to combine your skills, supplies, and resources. You will generate all sorts of creative and wonderful items from gourd scraps for head, hair, and ego ornament. Be creative and have fun. Be a Gourdhead!

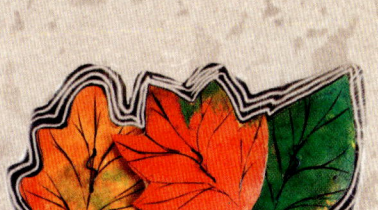

Gallery

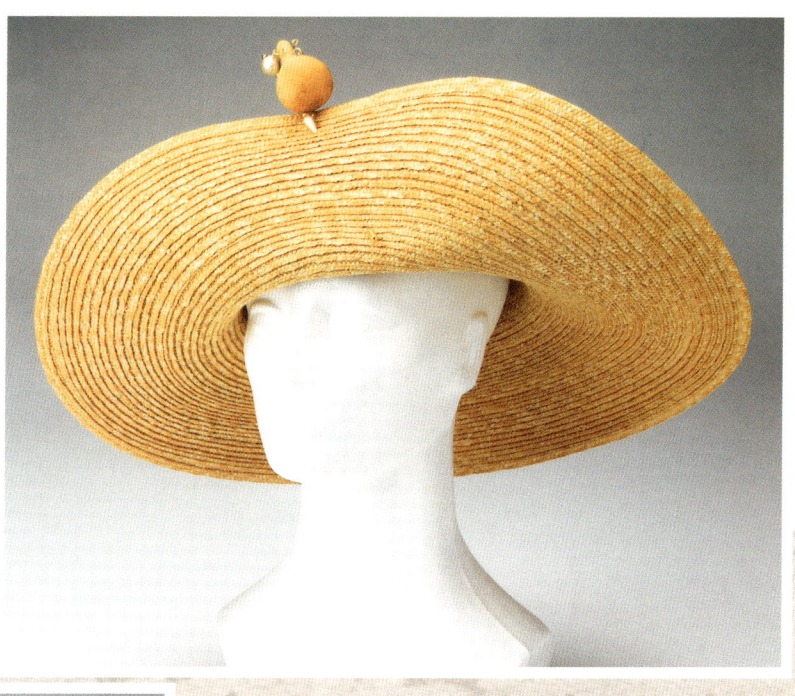

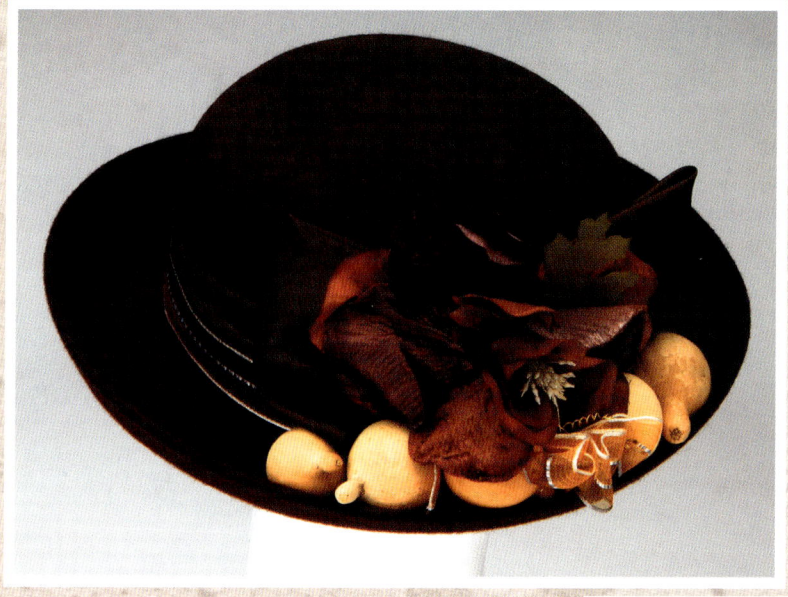

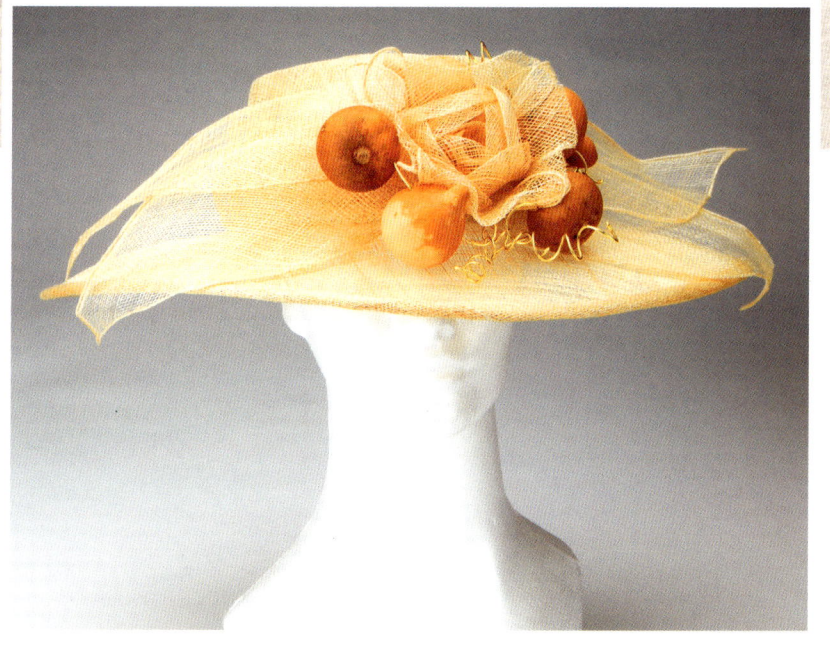

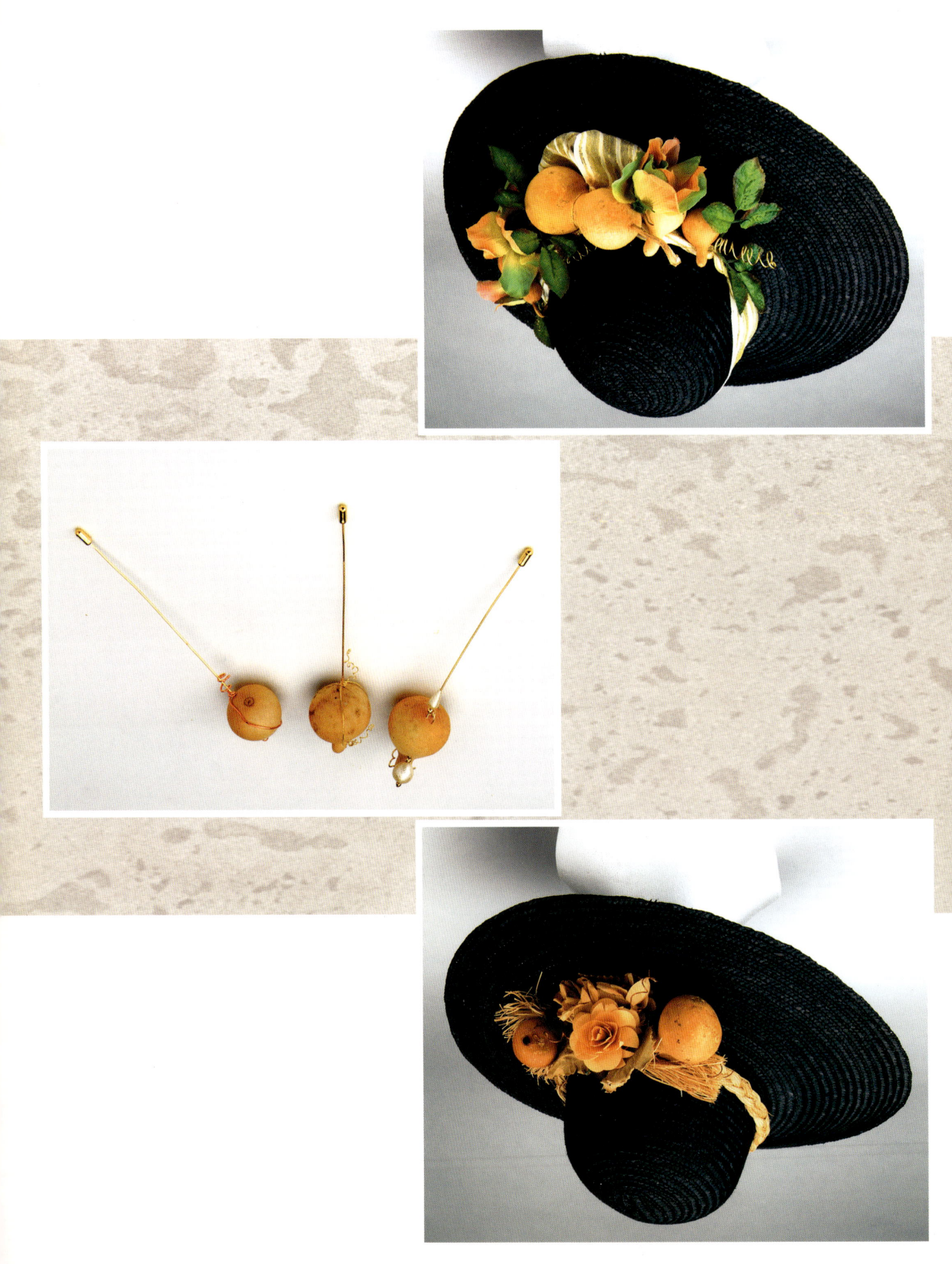

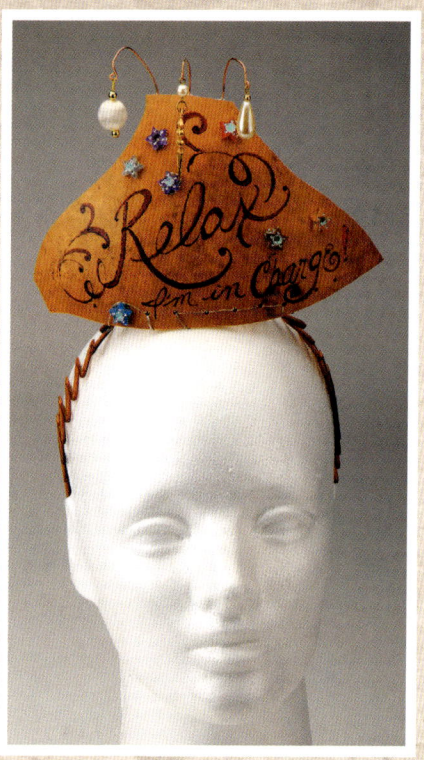

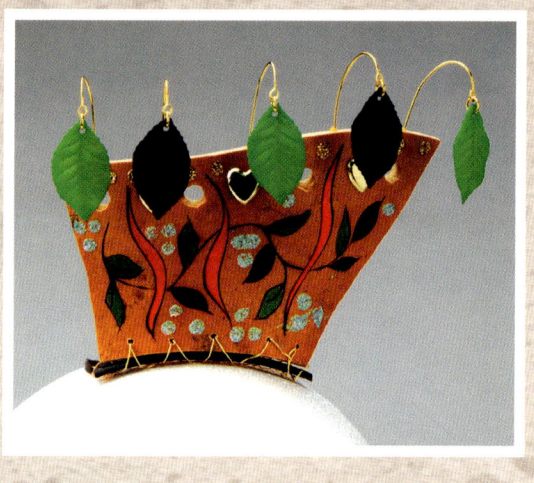

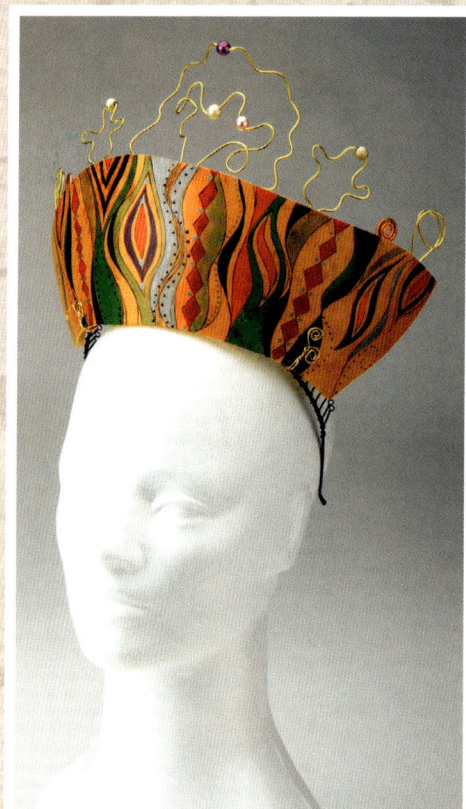

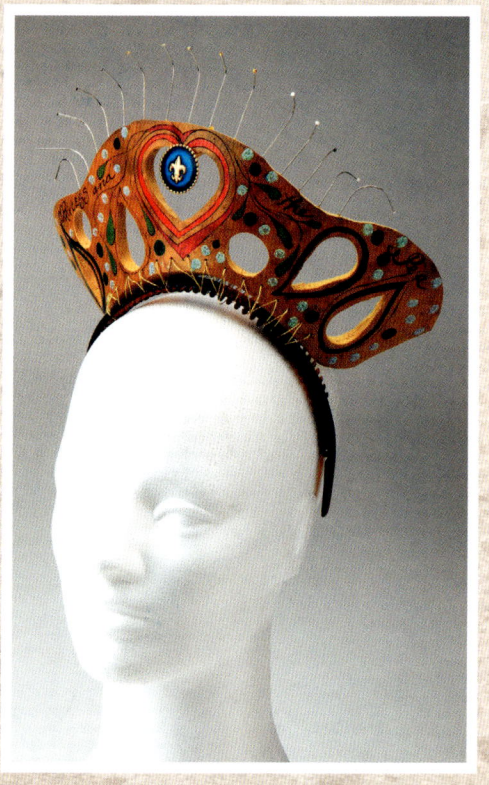

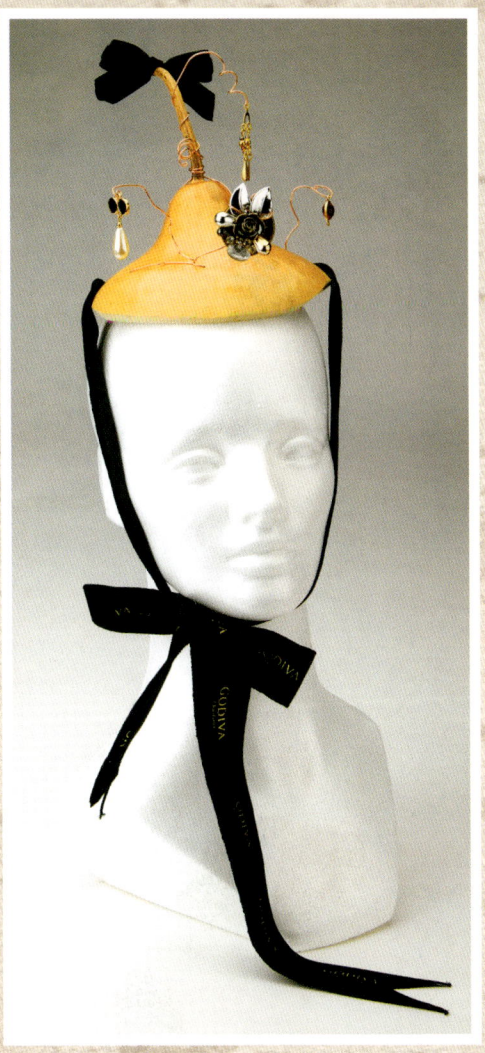

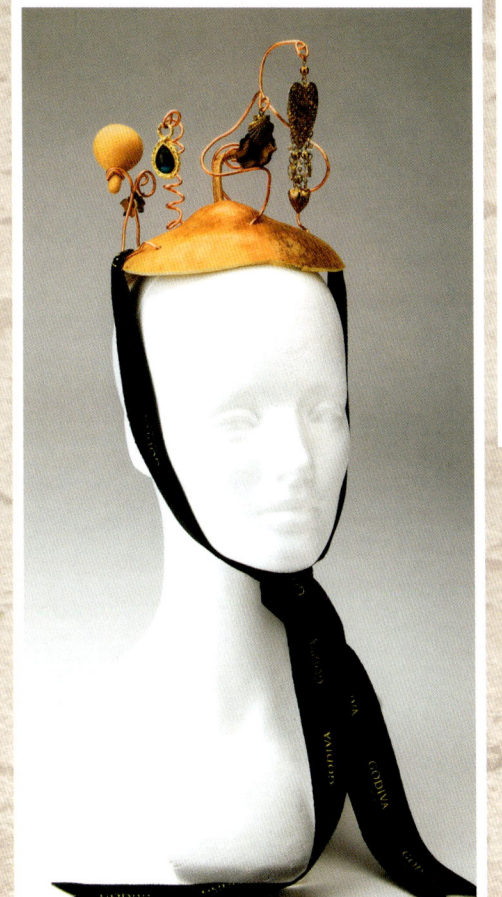

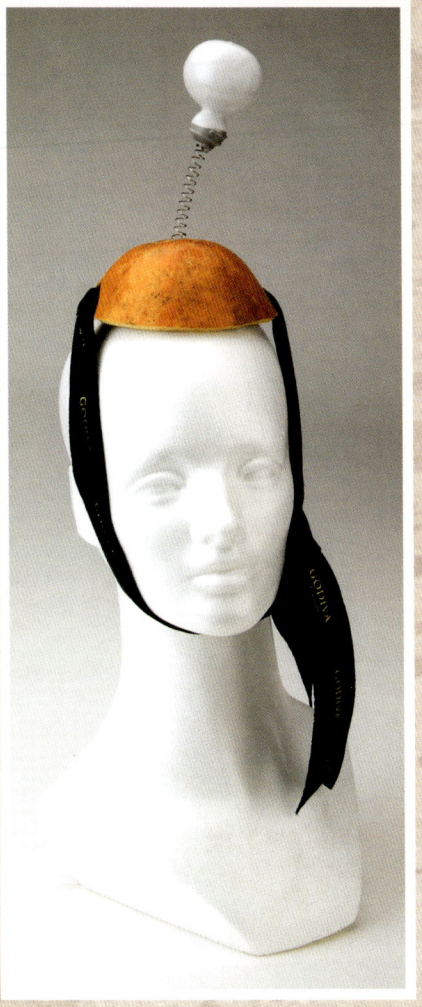

63

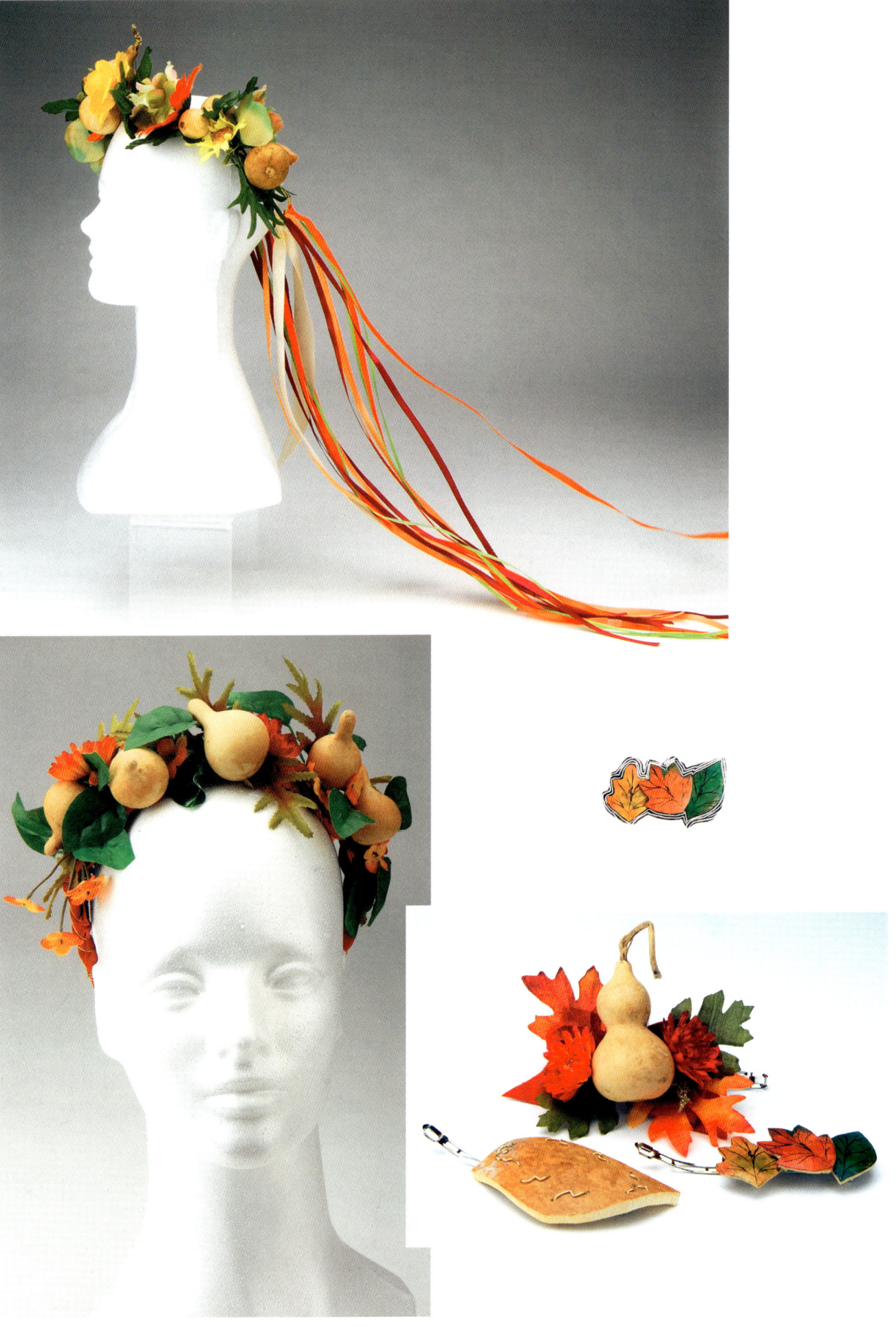